MARKETING FOR
SALESPEOPLE

How Servant Leadership Attracts Clients and Increases Sales

By Valdez Lasartemay

Table of Contents

Preface

In the vast landscape of sales, where every interaction is a potential tuuurning point, I find immense pleasure in introducing this guide, "Marketing for Salespeople: How Servant Leadership Attracts Clients and Increases Sales." As the architect of these pages, I extend my heartfelt gratitude to the legion of sales professionals who have graced my professional journey, imparted invaluable lessons, and shaped the contours of my own selling experiences.

To my esteemed colleagues, mentors, and collaborators—thank you for the shared insights, the triumphs celebrated together, and the challenges navigated side by side. Your collective wisdom has been the compass guiding me through the dynamic realms of salesmanship, and I am indebted to each of you for contributing to the mosaic of knowledge that forms the foundation of this book.

"Marketing for Salespeople" is a culmination of years spent honing the craft of selling, navigating the intricate dance between supply and demand, and forging lasting connections with clients. It is a testament to the collective expertise of those who have walked the sales terrain before me, leaving imprints of wisdom that have helped me navigate the ever-evolving landscape of marketing.

As you embark on this journey through the pages of this book, envision it as a shared expedition, a collaborative venture inspired by the rich tapestry of experiences etched by the collective efforts of the sales community. It is my sincere hope that the insights encapsulated within these chapters will not only serve as a reflection of our shared endeavors but also as a guiding light for your individual pursuits.

To the reader, whether you are a seasoned sales professional, a budding marketer, or an aspiring entrepreneur, I extend an invitation to immerse yourself in the transformative potential of these pages. This book is crafted with the belief that within its contents lie the keys to unlocking new dimensions in your sales journey. It is a reservoir of strategies, methodologies, and perspectives that have been refined through the crucible of real-world sales scenarios.

May "Marketing for Salespeople" be the catalyst for profound growth in your professional trajectory. May it empower you to not only attract ideal clients but also to refine your approach, elevate your marketing acumen, and, if your aspirations dare, traverse the path of entrepreneurship with newfound confidence.

As you delve into the chapters that follow, remember that you are not merely reading a book; you are engaging in a dialogue with the collective wisdom of those who have shaped the discourse of sales. Embrace the possibilities, absorb the lessons, and let the journey begin.

With gratitude and anticipation,

Valdez Lasartemay

Author, "Marketing for Salespeople: How Servant Leadership Attracts Clients and Increases Sales."

TIME FOR A CHANGE

PART 01

Dear Future Sales Leaders,

Did you know approximately 84% of consumers trust recommendations from people they already know? I have sold and managed salespeople for over 20 years. I am writing this book because as a manager who has worked hard to develop top salespeople, I learned that the biggest challenge my salespeople faced was the shortage of quality people to talk to.

My book is different from anything you have seen, because it focuses on branding sales professionals who are relationship builders, who are consultative, or needs-based in their selling approach. These types of salespeople will be helped by adding marketing savvy to their skillset. Marketing and sales sometimes get confused with each other, but they are two different animals. Sales involves helping prospective clients or customers by listening to them and understanding their wants and needs, to find them what they are looking for. Marketing educates and engages the customer by satisfying their needs while simultaneously positioning the service provider as a trusted advisor and source. If you are in needs-based sales, focus on being fiduciaries for your clients. Being a synergistic sales and marketing professional suits you.

Referral marketing is the original organic marketing method and the foundation when it comes to marketing for salespeople. When more than 80% of buyers trust their peer's recommendations, and only 29% of sales professionals are proactive in referral marketing, this will demonstrate a huge, missed opportunity. Not only can you capitalize on this, but you will prosper continually when you recognize you are the owner of Relationship Capital so that you can first develop, then manage to create greater leverage and rewards for yourself. To do so, you will need a new paradigm.

PART 02

I have trained good salespeople who did well when they had qualified prospects to talk to but were dependent on the company to supply them with leads.

When the marketing was off or when the economy shifted, their business just dried up. During a market downturn, I fired a lot of potentially good salespeople. Why? Because they were not good at lead generation and relied on cold calling. I had one woman cry when I let her go. She felt she was good at what she was doing—she just did not have enough prospects. She did not promote herself very well and relied on company marketing, which was zero at the time. I would say that laying people off was the toughest part of my job. I could not sleep the night before. We kept the good ones, who would not? I was not responsible for the turnover, but I felt bad just the same.

So, I thought to myself, how could I hire better, train better and manage better? My conclusion was to focus on training better. Instead of allowing my salespeople to continue to rely on company lead generation and other inefficient tactics to reach prospects, I could serve them better by teaching them how to create leads on their own. I looked at how I succeeded when I was in the same situation. I did not even know that my referral business was as strong as it was, until I became a manager and had the opportunity to look at my salespeople's businesses and see what they were doing and not doing.

In reading this book as a salesperson, you will benefit from seeing yourself in the proper light. Some of you may come to realize you are in the wrong profession, working for the wrong company or selling the wrong product.

For the sales professional who wants to be positioned properly, this book can help you take off and experience new heights. You just need to be committed and be willing to prove to the selling community that you can exercise high integrity in selling and reach the heights of top producer—joining the top 20, 10 and the top 1% in your company or industry.

The process begins when you learn how to identify and optimize your secret wealth. Meaning, learn how to leverage your relationship capital to flatten out the rollercoaster ride known as the sales cycle. You want to read this book if you want to truly do what is right for your client, yourself and your company and succeed.

PART 03

What you will find in this book is a chance for you to get naked and take a good look at yourself and see what you bring to the table in your career. If you are weak in certain areas, you will assess whether you should improve that skill or circumvent it. You will learn how to fix areas you struggle in, but only if there is merit in doing so.

If you are strong in key skill sets but not being rewarded for your efforts, you will learn how to fix that too. You will take a hard look at who you should be talking to, about the value you provide, and who you should not be talking to as much.

My promise to you is that if you have integrity, you will learn how to magnify your value and increase your influence with the people who can help you and take a load of pressure off you.

I am going to help you connect the dots by allowing you to brand yourself through introspection. When you are clear on your value, you will get better at self-promotion and targeting the right clients and referral partners. You will find value in gaining a new focus which will help you direct energy where it is appreciated.

When I started to investigate ways to solve the lead generation problem for my salespeople, I was shocked to discover how many salespeople are content with getting the occasional referral, rather than becoming astute at referral marketing. The data is even more damning when you look at the ratio of referrals compared to referrals solicited. Unknowingly, I built my

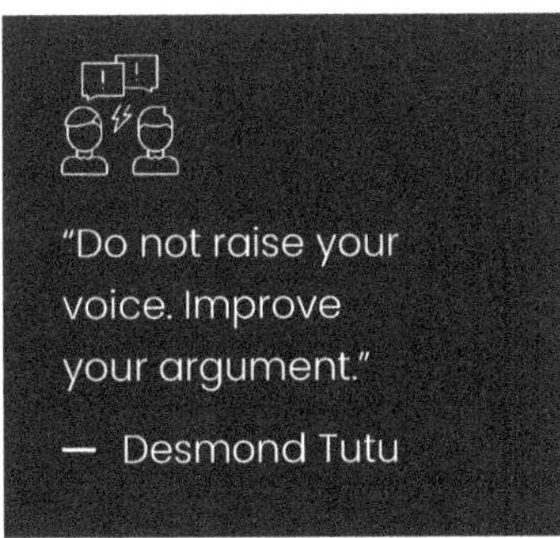

entire business on referrals; probably because I love leverage and I have been excellent at customer service and decent at self-promotion. I have seen terrible referral programs and some smart ways to create a referral culture that continues to produce results. In my investigation into the subject, I picked up additional ways to enhance relationships and business at the same time. I decided to write a book about my experience and share my insights after I took a deep dive into the subject. The mantra for most of the selling community has been ABC "always be closing." The new breed of

synergistic salespeople in my tribe are shifting to a different type of ABC and attracting better clients. This new breed does not need aggression and does not make a lot of noise. It breeds beliefs in increasing their value. A change could do you good!

CHAPTER
02
THE LIMITING BELIEF MOST SELLERS HAVE ABOUT THEIR RELATIONSHIPS

PART 01

In looking for a better way to manage my sales team, I took surveys of not only the salespeople who reported directly to me, but as many as I could reach within the company. I surveyed a good-sized segment of salespeople in a Fortune 500 Company.

I noticed that most of them believed their sales skills were at par. Most of the salespeople felt they did not need any sales training, per say. They felt that when they had clients in front of them, they had no problem getting them to either commit to buying or helping prospects decide the product was not right for them.

This group of salespeople did not feel like they were leaving anything on the table in their dealings with clients. The overwhelming consensus of the salespeople was that they were not getting enough leads. But this may or may not have been the only problem.

There was consistent complaining about the lack of marketing or marketing that just produced tire kickers. I am sure a good percentage of tire kickers buy because otherwise, the marketing dollars would go away.

This marketing department frequently used gifts for appointments. The sales force perspective was that these type of incentive programs just encourage freebie seekers to show up and waste the salesperson's time.

The marketing department was able to show me that they were bringing in more money than they were spending on marketing, and so they were happy.

Obviously, there was a disconnection in how the marketing was working. A closer look showed me that in different markets, the experience was quite different. In some markets, the gift for appointment yielded sales we would not have seen without the gifts.

In other markets, the salespeople were overwhelmed by freebie seekers. You must look at the strength of the sales professional and the territory. All the variables matter. A weak salesperson will not be helped by marketing.

The problem, as I see it, is, a salesperson who has wide fluctuations in sales correlating with company marketing is not a complete sales professional. The high and low sales were the result of many issues, but universally, the salespeople were not self-sufficient.

Through my own research, I learned there is a disconnection in a lot of companies across the country when it comes to this very issue. Marketing departments and sales forces often are on two different pages. Their ideas of what success looks like are different.

I also learned that some of the most successful selling organizations in the country have marketing departments and sales divisions that communicate often. These companies have developed a unified front. They have figured out a solution to this problem. Companies who coordinate sales and marketing efforts have better employee morale when it comes to their salespeople and marketing departments.

The two departments communicate and meet often. I do not know if salespeople spoke directly to the marketing department, or if sales managers and marketing managers came together, but their concerns were heard and addressed. Generally, the best-selling companies who had everything clicking had efficient communication between sales and marketing departments.

Unfortunately, most of the companies out there who hire salespeople are looking for salespeople to solve all their problems and save the company in some respects. A lot of companies either do a poor job of marketing, or they do not market at all. When they do market, it is an institutionalized marketing where they just put their brand out there.

Many companies try to create awareness with few effective calls to action. They may not even create incentives to come in and meet with the salespeople. There is a dichotomy where companies who do not market need aggressive persuasive salespeople to stay in business. Then there are companies who are particularly good at marketing and do not need sales professionals; they hire order takers.

When there is no marketing, salespeople are taught to be aggressive and experts at hard closing by using gimmicks and so forth. This creates a stressful environment because you get a lot of customers who buy, but then they cancel, renege, or whatever they do—they just fail to go through with the purchase.

Consumers will buy sometimes because salespeople are aggressive or pushy. They will buy just to get the salesperson to go away, and then find a way to return the product without dealing with the salesperson. For the salespeople who work in an environment where aggressive selling is the approach, you see a higher-than-average turnover. Often, you find salespeople who frequently misrepresent themselves and their companies, trying to make something happen.

All in all, the solution is to teach salespeople how to become servant leaders and synergistic sales and marketing experts. This approach is best in selling situations using a needs-based approach, not aggressive ride or die types.

There are many aspects involved in marketing. But salespeople do not need to learn the entire realm of what it means to be a marketer. They do not need to become a graphic designer or an expert copywriter.

What they need to focus on as a foundation is referral marketing. The key is to identify ideal clients, and then develop and manage relationships.

My synergistic sales and marketers become experts in Relationship Capital Management. But before even discussing relationship capital management, we need to learn how to develop relationships strategically to support our desired outcome, which is a business driven 80% by referrals.

And the first major objective for salespeople is to learn how to improve their customer service skills. They need to know how to create positive word of mouth, and how to become savvy at attracting and collecting referrals.

Sadly, when I ask salespeople if they are getting referrals, most of them are not honest with themselves. Without hesitation, many answer, "Yeah, I get plenty of referrals." Um, that is not really the truth.

They are getting the wrong referrals. They are getting referrals from people who may not have been very profitable—the occasional friend.

They get referrals from clients who have negotiated all the profit from sales. The problem with this is that they bring more of the same. When this is the case, referrals can leave a bad taste in the salesperson's mouth. This type of referral can hurt your business.

The hurdle salespeople must overcome if they want to improve their experience in selling and build more success in their business is deciding to learn a new but powerful skill set.

This decision requires taking a hard look at who they are in terms of their personality and how they resonate with their client base, the personality of their prospects, their product knowledge, and the company culture.

The sales professional might end up having to leave the firm they are with just to be in a situation where they can sell in a needs-based approach and start making better connections with the right type of clients. Selling this way will require change, but the long-term benefits make it worth it. It all begins with self-analysis.

PART 02

The new age of synergistic salespeople will continue to evolve, as companies continue to use institutionalized marketing. Institutionalized marketing is the practice of promoting only the company. When the company's focus is on the promotion of the company name and a catchy slogan or jingle, they are effectively increasing awareness of their company and products. The leads that trickle down to commissioned salespeople are random and unqualified.

My contention is that salespeople take matters into their own hands as a profession and do more than traditional prospecting i.e., cold calling, knocking on doors and leveraging their natural markets. They are just going to have to learn how to create business on their own.

An example of an unfortunate business development practice often occurs within many insurance companies. What they do is they hire a lot of young salespeople and sales agents that go through the whole process of getting licensed and learning about insurance products. And then they are asked to write down 250 people that they know.

To help jog their memories, they are asked to write who they may be able to contact from elementary school from church, from college, from high school, and all their relatives. And then they contact all these folks and let them know they are in the business and sell some of them. When they have gone through their lists, a lot of them are just out of business, out of luck, and out of a job.

A lot of the sales that the new agent made stay on the books long after the failed new insurance agent has left the company, giving up residual income. The insurance company wins.

It looks like some of these insurance companies have made turnover profitable and built these tactics into their marketing plans. They are constantly hiring people just to capture what sticks in the books while the new salespeople struggle to make it. It is cost effective since they are not paying them anything.

The new hires are usually on straight commission. They initially make a few sales, and then when they cannot fill their calendar, they stop selling and quit.

The company benefits because they get to keep the business that stays on the books; and then the company starts the cycle all over again and hires more salespeople.

It is cruel to me because the young guy embarrasses himself; the people that bought from him did so because of their relationship, or they needed the product, and not only that, but they also bought because they want the kid to succeed.

When family and friends look for him a year later, they will find out that the kid is no longer with that company. A good amount of this business stays on the books.

It often does not benefit the acquaintances of the new kid to cancel their relationship with the company because there may be tax consequences. This is not a smart way to do business, but it works.

What could be better is if these salespeople learned more than just presentation skills and product knowledge and learn how to develop their relationship capital. They are taught to ask for referrals, but the training is weak.

What they need to learn is how referral marketing done correctly will continue to bring them leads over a long period of time and sustain them in their business. Some of the newly hired salespeople either do this naturally or have strong networks from the start. The real crime is, a lot of times, if you do not have what the insurance company calls a strong natural market of people who have disposable income, you are going to go out of business very quickly.

The less fortunate sales agent spends an ordinate amount of time and effort cold calling or knocking on doors which seems punitive, but people do succeed at building their businesses this way. You can succeed this way because it makes you tough, but it is not fun. It is just like rubbing your knuckles and feet on concrete or burning a hole in your ears.

Cold calling is not ideal. My vision is to improve the profession by developing salespeople who are intrapreneurs. They will even become entrepreneurs. My objective is to train sales professionals to be marketers and then have them take complete ownership for creating their own leads. My protégés work strategically and are conscious about where they can expect the business to come from long term.

It is just a better way to grow. The insurance industry is unique because they use a combination of institutional advertising and natural marketing.

In other industries, a natural market does not make sense and makes building relationships even more critical. At least with insurance, you can succeed right away if you sustain yourself the first year and set things up properly.

It is just a waste of human relationship capital to turn over salespeople by not setting them up to succeed. I attribute the turnover to a lack of the right type of training. There is a better way.

PART 03

To give you the best opportunity to succeed regardless of race, gender, or social status, I will teach you how to brand yourself and how to create and deliver high value to the markets you serve.

A tough career decision might be necessary for the existing sales professionals depending on how you respond to some deeply personal questions in your own self-analysis and identifying your dream clients.

If you like the selling opportunity you currently have, ask yourself if you are with the right company or if you are selling the right product. Are you selling to the right audience? You want to be enthusiastic about all the above. If you answered yes, you are all set and ready to fine tune what you are already doing. You must believe you have a good match. If you have issues with any of the above, you will figure out what you need to do after completing the self-analysis coming up in the chapters that follow.

It does not hurt for all of us to look at our businesses and careers; not only at the start, but periodically to see if we are progressing or spinning our wheels.

An introspective look at what you are currently doing will help you figure out if you can make your current career work. Or give you directions for adjusting. You may see opportunities to better manage your time and collaborate more efficiently with your existing clients. We will go over what you might do later in this book.

Be forewarned; when you look under the microscope at your current process, you might find out that you are in the wrong profession, or you are with the wrong company. You may feel you need to change who you are talking to in terms of prospects.

If you feel you should make a change, do so with confidence. Evaluating your current situation is easy, and you will be given tools to do so in this book.

It takes some work to get it all straightened out in your mind. But the result will be that you are going to have a much more fulfilling career.

You are going to do a much better job serving your clients. And regardless of what your company does for lead generation, you will become indispensable to your company. More importantly, you will become indispensable to the clients you develop, when you develop them the right way.

When you improve your level of service, you improve your value. By getting more involved in your client's business, you will create a strong reputation and positive word of mouth advertising. Eventually, you will attract more of the type of clients that you really like to do business with.

There are a lot of other benefits as well when you begin taking a different look at your sales career and seeing yourself as an intrapreneur.

Are you up to the task? Are you willing to do the work? You cannot imagine putting more work on your plate. Initially, you need to go above and beyond with the belief that the hard part is during your take off and that once you reach high altitude, you can coast.

Often, great achievements are only one decision away. When you are working with a clear purpose and know what your intentions are, work and play will begin to blur.

Being a fiduciary for your clients is enriching for you and your company. This approach prepares you for being a top producer in your company. Maybe even setting you up for owning your own business; leading your way into the C suite as CEO. It is common for star sales professionals to become eventual CEOs, because they have learned what makes the customers tick!

When you take a deep dive into your business, you gain insights as to what is truly needed in communicating to your markets. No longer will you be the average salesperson armed with canned presentation skills and basic product knowledge.

No longer will you be just a player in the game—the game will change, and you will be the game changer. You may develop great influence and become a game changer for a lot of people too.

You will differentiate yourself because you impact people in a different way. It is a beautiful thing because there is nothing better than being able to give such high-level service, going above and beyond what your company even intended.

A major intangible benefit is the intrinsic reward you receive while providing excellent service to the best of your clients. Your newfound ability to target the best clients and attract them to you eliminates your need to depend on company leads ever again.

CHAPTER
03
FIRST IMPRESSIONS—
YOU ARE THE MESSAGE

PART 01

As a sales professional, you are the message. Marshall McLuhan said the medium is the message. In this case, you are the medium to which sales messages are being delivered. Your first impression often is the only impression you will make.

In my selling career, a suit and tie were the minimum standard dress code for men. How you dress really depends on the industry and expectations of the market you serve.

Violating dress code or the expectations for dress code is risky. I know there's temptation to exercise your taste in fashion. Some salespeople might even go as far as saying that they are not going to compromise their identities or forego their body jewelry, tattoos, or their fashionable hairstyles.

Many salespeople feel they do not want to be sellouts and question the issue of being authentic and true to themselves when it comes to appearances. I am not going to tell you that you must change any of that, but I will tell you that The Platinum Rule really holds true here. Simply put, consider your audience. I will give you great details about the strategy behind The Platinum Rule in Chapter six.

It is not about you! It is about your ideal clients. If your ideal clients will not buy from you because of whatever it is that you do to express your uniqueness, you are shooting yourself in the foot.

Some might say, "Well I don't want to sell out." Yes, you do. If you want to be a servant leader, you must present yourself the way that your market expects.

Cultural or ethnic influences on your attire may or may not have an impact on your performance. One thing I love about marketing is the reliance on collecting data, trying different approaches, and evaluating the results. The numbers do not lie. You can evaluate the market, but I think playing it safe is your best option.

I want to share a quick story to give you some more insight into this issue. In Santa Barbara, California, I was having a hard time finding a registered representative to hire for the bank I was representing.

Finally, I received a resume that looked good on paper, and I scheduled an interview. To my surprise, the male interviewee wore a ponytail.

I was concerned about this candidate being a good fit. Human resources said I had to hire him if he was qualified, but my manager hated the idea. The staff in Santa Barbara insisted he would fit in because many of their customers wore ponytails, as this was a beach community and the norm.

The manager at that bank told me it was not going to be an issue because most of their clientele were wealthy beach-bum type looking people and that he would fit right in.

My team looked at me like I was crazy to even think about bringing a guy in who wore a ponytail. In fact, my HR department told me I cannot tell him what to do with his hair because it would be a violation.

My corporate management advised me to tell him to cut his hair before he showed up in our corporate office for training.

So, I hired him, and I told him to cut his hair. He cut off about 1/2 inch, but still wore a ponytail—not a great improvement.

I was caught in the middle of corporate conservatism and the politically correct human resource department.

Because I initiated a conversation with human resources, I was forced to give him a shot. He was qualified for the job on paper, and he felt the same way.

As it turns out, he failed. There may be more than one reason he failed, but I deduced from the situation that the main reason he failed was because in that market, even though they wore ponytails, they did not want to invest their money with somebody who wore one.

This prejudice is because they expected someone who managed their money to look like they came from Wall Street.

A segment of this market did wear cargo shorts, T-shirts, ponytails and enjoyed that attire. The catch is this, they did not want their investment advisor looking like that because they associated whatever you associate with someone who has a hang loose attitude.

Valid or not, people make assumptions about you. But you have control over how you are perceived to a certain extent. Do not make it hard on yourself.

This market did not want someone who looked carefree and relaxed managing their investment portfolio. Markets can be fickle this way.

When I was a producing sales representative, I had a similar surprise. Being of African American decent, I hesitated to take over a territory in the country where the population was rural and Caucasian. The market was under served and it was an opportunity for sure, but I was not sure how I would be received.

I did very well and proved my own reservations were not valid. I do not want to tell people how they should look, but you do not get to make that decision.

Sometimes, selling in different markets, different territories, or selling different products all make a difference. You could easily be selling in a saturated market and blame yourself using whatever excuse you can manufacture. The issue may or may not be you though.

Your knowledge of yourself enhanced, by using The Platinum Rule and Servant Leadership will solve most of your sales and marketing challenges.

PART 02

Attitude makes all the difference in the world. I contend that you have no choice but to have a positive attitude.

You should be extremely optimistic. Imagine if you are going to war and you had a choice between being optimistic or pessimistic about the outcome, I am here to tell you that optimism will serve you a lot better than being pessimistic.

Fear can consume you if you allow it, so given the choice, be optimistic.

I am not saying that you should be pollyannaish and lose sight of reality.

You cannot look at a situation that is grim and give yourself a bunch of positive affirmations and expect that everything is going to be okay.

That is not what I am saying at all. I am saying if you are going to win, if you are going to play, expect to win.

Colin Powell once said, "Optimism is a Force Multiplier." Well, you must dig a little deeper into what he is saying. He is using military terms. What he is really saying is that if you are attacking your opponent from the front and the rear and you are flanking them from both sides, you should be optimistic because you have solid strategy and tactics to get the job done.

You cannot just create optimism out of thin air; you must be competent. Competency translates into confidence, and if you are competent, you have every reason in the world to be optimistic.

There must be something behind your optimism. When you look at your skill set and you identify your strong points and utilize them, you are operating from a position of strength.

When your strong points are appreciated in one market and not the other, you simply direct yourself towards the market that you best serve.

You have reason to be optimistic. In chapter four, you will look at your personal assessment, your Strengths, Weaknesses, Opportunities and Threats, or SWOT for short. You have an opportunity to see where you may have some gaps in your knowledge and opportunities to gain experience. You then improve your chances for success by working to fill those gaps. Competency brings confidence. Be optimistic and be a realist at the same time.

If you follow boxing in the United States, you have heard of Mike Tyson. I would like to use him as an example when it comes to optimism. Mike Tyson was intimidating; he had a history of hurting other boxers and knocking them out in less than three rounds.

The first fight I want to use to illustrate the power of optimism was against Michael Spinks. In that fight, it was obvious that the fight was over before it started.

Michael Spinks saw the early success of Mike Tyson when he was knocking out opponents left and right. You could see in Michael Spinks eyes before the fight that he was scared to death; his fear consumed him totally. The fight did not last long—he was knocked out immediately.

Some people say Mike Tyson would have knocked Spinks out in any scenario because Tyson was stronger, had more power, etc.

Not true. Spinks was a smaller man, but he was a better athlete with great stamina. And although it was not evident at the time, Mike Tyson had a respiratory issue, he lacked stamina. The longer the fight lasted, the higher the chances of Tyson losing.

Michael Spinks did not have a chance because he was defeated in his mind. Spinks could not see himself winning. It was obvious he had no plan or strategy—he must have been hoping for a miracle. He knew he could not out-punch Tyson early in the fight, yet he tried and lost.

Had he known his strengths and weaknesses, he would have avoided a punching match and made the fight drag on to the latter rounds where his stamina would give him a chance. He may not have known Tyson's weaknesses, but the conclusion for Spinks could have been different had he focused on his strengths instead of his weaknesses. Do not let that be you.

In another Mike Tyson fight, he fights an unknown boxer, Buster Douglas. Buster had recently lost a parent and was grieving. Buster Douglas did not have time to psyche himself out of winning or losing; he was grieving a parent.

Buster was flabby and looked out of shape. He was not very skillful, nothing notable about him, but he was big enough to have a punchers' chance. Also, he had none of the athletic ability of Michael Spinks.

If you know anything about boxing, you know that Buster Douglas beat Mike Tyson up.

The reason that happened is because the death of a parent changes you. It changes you permanently but when you first experience it, your mind is not functioning in a normal way.

Buster Douglas did not have the ability to be afraid. He was in another place, he just focused on the target in front of him.

Succeeding is a mind game, but it is real. When you do not allow fear to control your mind, when you stop pessimism; you give yourself an advantage.

Mike Tyson took Buster Douglas for granted; in fact, he shortchanged his own preparation for that fight. The result was, he lost badly. Mike Tyson lost more than a fight. He no longer intimidated anyone after this loss. But Tyson is a true champion. Throughout his life, he has had to fight tremendous adversity and loss, yet he continues to move forward. After boxing, he found a way to become a successful brand and business success.

There are multiple reasons why this fight did not work out for him, but I want to focus on his opponent. Buster Douglas did not fear him because he was grieving; and when you are grieving, fear is something that you just do not experience.

In both boxing examples, the difference between victory and loss was mental. What you think about yourself brings about the result. If you feel overwhelmed and fear you are over your head, you need to work on your strategy and your skills.

Your competence is the foundation for confidence, not wishful thinking. A positive attitude will give you a better chance than a negative one.

When you maintain your focus and learn to shut out the noise telling you are not good enough to reach your goals, you continue to advance. You may not be able to eliminate feelings of doubt completely, but you can choose to be courageous and move forward despite your fear.

Buster Douglass is worthy of studying because he was forced to close his mind to the noise that all of us hear when we are striving to advance. Buster did not choose to manage his thinking; he was unfortunately stunned by the loss of a parent. You do not have to lose a parent to develop tunnel vision. You can decide at any time you are going to focus on the task at hand, the task right in front of you. You just make the decision!

As you advance in your career, your experience and your competence are continually improving. Your business and your income should too.

That is why playing the long game makes all the sense in the world. Establishing a strong foundation by selecting the right product, the right audience and the right niche within that audience gives you an advantage. Over time, you will dominate your niche.

We're building one piece at a time—we're building a tremendous opportunity for ourselves when we follow the steps I've given you in this text.

Muhammad Ali, another boxer, says, "A man who thinks the same at age 20 as he does at age 50 has wasted 30 years of his life."

Learn something every day and be focused on the things that matter.

I would suggest to the realist who thinks that optimism is a waste of time that great advancements in our society have all been born from the imagination and the belief that dreams can become reality with a plan.

I encourage you to know your personal reality and be optimistic that you can grow. Document your daily results using customer relationship management software. Understand your sales numbers to determine where your business is coming from. Focus on the top 20% of your clients who give you the most business and referrals, hence, your optimism will be warranted.

When you have numbers to support your actions, you will see the difference between being blindly optimistic and being logistical.

Now, if you are struggling at the very beginning because you have a hill to climb and you have a lot of skills in need of improvement, I suggest you work every day on your opportunities to improve. Be strategic in what you prioritize using the tools in this book. Remember the beginning of your journey is often the toughest.

In the process, you should use positive affirmations every day. Stand in front of the mirror after you brush your teeth and tell yourself "I am in it to win it. I am committed to learning what I need to learn to make myself the professional that I dream of being." Use your own words for the best results but work on your thinking every day.

As a synergistic sales professional/marketer or anyone who engages in any type of entrepreneurial activity, understand that you have two voices: the voice of the angel and the voice of the demon.

Often, what happens is that, when your angel voice tells you can succeed, only minutes later, that demon voice tells you all the reasons why you cannot.

Understand that every single successful person has had to manage this process, and that you are not the exception. You have permission not to listen to negativity; in fact be aware this will happen and deal with it by forcing more positive thinking into your mindset.

Deliberately focus on your positive affirmations. improve your skillset daily and make sure your positive voice is based on you doing the work; eventually, you will laugh at your negative voice.

What you are going to find is you are going to grow into the person that you aspire to be, and you are going to reduce your own internal negative talk in the process.

PART 03

In summary, you are responsible for putting yourself together, both mentally and physically. You are also putting together your market, and so there's work involved. Just do the work.

The work will become easier as you grow, because you are aligning yourself with your personality and purposeful goals, and you are serving your chosen market. Soon, everything will start to click.

If you are going to work hard, you might as well work at something that is close to your heart and is in line with your natural gifts, your personality, and your talents. If you have personality quirks like fashion statements or body jewelry and so forth, that might inhibit your career. You may need to make a tough decision.

Focus on The Platinum Rule in chapter six and learn that it is not about you, you are a servant leader.

The word 'servant' can take on many meanings. If you get hung up on the word, substitute it with leadership. Just know that great leaders were first, great followers.

The reality is that if you serve your markets at a high level, you are going to be the leader in that market. And that is what we are shooting for—getting you to a place where you are dominant.

What you are doing is mastering marketing to a segment of your industry, and who knows, you may grow much further. I honestly believe that the tools you are being given here are exactly what you need to make you a powerhouse.

Be diligent at completing your SWOT (Strengths, Weaknesses, Opportunities and Threats) analysis in the next chapter. Look at who you are as a person, look at the people you serve and embody your personal goals by making them your life's mission, and you cannot help but persevere. I used plenty of boxing references here. This is because when I think of champions, boxing comes to mind first. I am building champions. Champions are not measured by their wins; they are recognized by their willingness to pick themselves up and persevere. Every champion was once a contender who refused to give up.

Keep good notes, study those notes, and look at your life like a puzzle you have an opportunity to not only put together, but to design using ingredients unique to you! You are putting your life together so that all the pieces add up to you being the best version of yourself.

Your opportunity is serving the audience that appreciates you the most. Lift yourself up as high as you can, go riding the wave that is really you, you are riding on your own power—your personal power.

CHAPTER 04

BECOMING A SYNERGISTIC SALES AND MARKETING PROFESSIONAL

PART 01

The new paradigm is **Synergistic Sales and Marketing** (SSM). Becoming a synergistic sales and marketer, or SYNER for short, starts by first taking a close look at what you bring to the table. My suggestion is that you do what we call a SWOT analysis.

The first step is to define first what you are good at. Write down all your strong points, not only in relation to sales, but in relation to you as a human being and your personal interests. This is a brainstorming exercise, so leave no stone unturned. Here is a tip: think of times when you were the happiest. This usually coincides with times you were either performing at your best or having the time of your life. Documenting all this data will serve you in matching your unique personality to the right products, clients, companies, and will serve you in choosing the right type of personal goals.

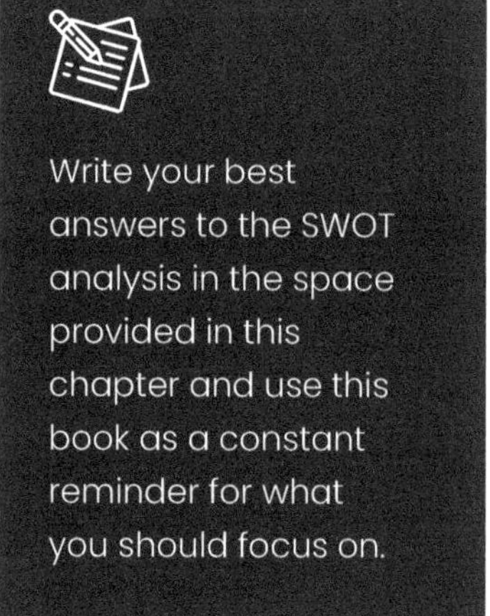

Next in our SWOT analysis is documenting weaknesses; areas of opportunity or areas you should delegate entirely. List all your weaknesses and if you struggle with this, ask your peers, your friends, and your family members about both your strengths and your weaknesses. We often come to know ourselves through the eyes of others. Our own perspective of ourselves is not necessarily shared by others. Somewhere in the mix of perceptions, is your personal truth. Because the more accurate you are, the better you will be at aligning yourself properly with both companies, products, and clients.

Intentionally left blank

Intentionally left blank

Now that you have documented your strengths and your weaknesses, look at your opportunities. Where do you think your best opportunities lie? Where are you under-utilizing your talent?

If you feel you are not where you should be in life, where would you like to see yourself? Where do you think you might fit in best? Also, think of the groups of people which you relate to at the highest level.

Lastly, look at anything that might come between you and your goals and list them as threats. Be clear to identify them because you want to produce strategies to minimize or prevent their influence on your progress.

Be discriminate. Discrimination is one of your best tactics when it comes to where you invest your energy and your time. You want to make sure that you are matching who you are as a person with your strongest suit. You want to align yourself with audiences and groups of people who appreciate you the most and most profitably.

Caution: In this exercise, you owe it to yourself to determine if your prejudices and or reservations for not being able to serve a given group of people is real, or something you need to work out in your head.

When it comes to salesmanship, you want to look at who you resonate with. Trying to be everything to everybody is a mistake.

Often, making a shift in the company you work for, the product you sell, or the audience you serve can make a huge difference in whether you are going to be successful or not. So do not leave any stone unturned when going through this exercise of evaluating your strong points, your weaknesses, your opportunities, and anything that you think might come in your way.

You may find that in doing this exercise, you may have to make a few tough decisions. If you are already involved in your career and discover you are not properly aligned with your values, you may have to make a change. If you are like me, you may have to make a change in geography. You might have to

pack your bags and move to where you are most appreciated.

Your SWOT analysis will help you in many ways including goal setting. You have heard of the SMART goal setting system. SMART is an acronym for a tool that helps us to make our goals realistic. Your goals should be Specific, Measurable, Achievable and Time bound. This is a smart approach to goal setting.

A goal is simply a dream with a deadline; and a dream without a fight is a nightmare.

The SMART approach to goals is great for showing you how to achieve goals you set for yourself once you start to make plans for leveraging the results of your SWOT analysis. While the SMART approach gives you methodology, the next chapter will help you select the right type of goals based on your unique qualities as a conscientious sales professional.

PART 02

Your SWOT analysis will also help you develop your own persona. Your knowledge of self makes it even more clear who you should connect with— "Birds of a feather flock together." All you need is a common thread, not the whole persona, but a common interest that can help you form an alliance.

Your starting point is to first embrace your key attributes. Working in your strongest suit makes work more enjoyable; and time will move fast when you enjoy what you are doing.

I do not encourage you to focus on strengthening your weaknesses unless they are critical to achieving your objective, just acknowledge them. There are people who will tell you that you should work on your weaknesses to round out your experience. I tend to disagree with that; I think that you should look at what your natural capabilities are and build on those. Why not collaborate with people who are strong where you are weak if you can.

By completing the SWOT analysis, you now know what your strong points are, focus on building and improving them. You have discovered your advantage; now you must constantly develop and improve your expertise.

Your newfound focus will help you match your strongest skills with opportunities that support them. You will begin to make more strategic and make better decisions.

You may decide to change where you are going to sell or what you are going to sell, and how you are going sell it. The goal is to improve your chances for success by improving your positioning.

You now could leverage your strongest attributes in serving your market and create language in all your communications to promote yourself. You can now be specific about what your best talent is and promote it like crazy.

You can set yourself apart and specialize. And with a little help from the relationship capital you are developing, find more and more opportunity to use your God given talent. There is no real advantage to being a generalist. It is nice to be well rounded, but not optimal to promote yourself as one. There is marketing power in being specific in the problems you solve best.

When you have a specialty, you are enthusiastic about that, and it pulls you instead of you having to push yourself. Ride the wave and go with that energy.

Specializing can make your life easier; working will be fun, and people will notice your enthusiasm. Hard work becomes less hard when you enjoy what you are doing.

Reflecting on the cliché "Do what you love, and the money will follow you" suggests that when you tap into your strongest suit, you will get stronger; and this cliché becomes true for you. When you are aligned properly, your life just becomes easier.

Your specialty should be able to solve a problem your market is trying to solve to ensure you have a large enough niche, and a large enough market to be able to keep yourself busy and profitable. When your specialty is in demand, set your goal for penetrating this market through relationship capital development and management.

Penetrate your market niche by focusing on those who need your solution and appreciate what you do. Once again, this is a type of discrimination. Being discriminate serves you best. It is not a selfish decision to do what you are best at with people who need and appreciate what you do most; it is smart!

Personal branding is smart because it is a better way of doing business. You might find that in a corporate environment, this approach may draw attention to you. However, no one will argue with you if you are exceeding your sales goals by being a specialist versus being a generalist.

Positioning yourself takes a little work; no one said it did not, but it is going to be work you enjoy doing. Be selfish and do what is best for you. If you move on to a different opportunity, stick with your plan. Do what you do best, and your outcome is going to be better. This, I promise you.

One thing you will discover is that because you specialize, you will find new and improved ways to talk about your product and the problems it solves and identify more audiences and improve your efficiency.

There are always different ways to explain and demonstrate. When you sell a given product as a specialist, you will find all the different nuances that improve your client appreciation for how you are solving their problems. You will know all the different angles and applications for your product.

Personal Branding

When we are identifying who we are as individuals in our SWOT analysis, or identifying our unique four personality traits, we cannot lose sight of our will. We have an opportunity to create our unique persona. Take your natural attributes and put yourself together the way you want to be recognized. Physical brands have associated themselves using slogans. Hertz was successful using "We try harder" as a slogan, positioning themselves uniquely despite being the second largest brand in their category. Coca Cola is always associated with the color red. Many entertainers are using monikers to be remembered instead of their full names. For example, "The Rock," "The Weekend," "Prince," "Madonna," "Cher," "Pitbull." All these monikers are readily known by their fans. James Earl Jones is known as the voice who has never shown his face portraying Darth Vader and other characterizations because of his unique sound. Your opportunity is to shape your unique persona using the attributes that both resonate with you and what you anticipate will set you apart in your market niche. Gather what you will learn from this chapter and the chapter on personality and ask yourself several introspective questions to help you create your brand. Remember, you must be consistent when branding yourself if you want your brand to stick! Conduct an audit: what qualities and skills do you possess? The obtained information will form the basis of your personal brand. Start, by deciding...

For what would I like to be known?

Do you have a favorite color that no matter what, you will wear something of that color?

Who should know about me?

How and to whom can my knowledge and skills be useful the most?

Who will get the most value from interacting with me?

What do I want people to say about me?

Remember all your public behavior must be consistent with the positioning that you have created in your branding.

PART 03

You now have a specialty in mind. And before you go full steam ahead, take the next step and size up the market for your special brand of salesmanship of your given special product or service.

The next step is to identify your ideal client, your IDC, for short. Are you up to the task? By going through your SWOT analysis, you have looked at yourself with introspection and looked at your strong points, your weaknesses, and so forth.

Now it is time to look at the needs of the ideal client that you would like to serve. Are you able to bring value above and beyond with this type of client? Is the problem you solve widespread enough to support your business if you create enough awareness through the strategies and tactics you are learning?

When you see the opportunity clearly and find it viable, you can begin evaluating your theory. At the outset, you will position yourself as the 'Go to Guy,' their fiduciary.

If you are not ready yet, you at least know what you need to do. Close any knowledge gaps you may have and become the resource your clients need.

This is work you can achieve because you are matching your skill set with your chosen audience, and you know what they need. They appreciate what you bring to the table. Now it is up to you to increase your value and make it clear that you are the resource they need to accomplish their goals.

If you are there already, great! But if not, do not despair. You know what you need to do to get there, so going forward, look at your ideal client and study what their needs are, as well as their hopes and their desires.

Then devote yourself to helping them achieve their goals. You can get clarity by asking clients what their greatest challenges are. Play detective and ask yourself, what are the questions no one is asking? Talk to people close to the business or the client and look for inefficiencies and put people and solutions together by being innovative.

Leverage the rapport you have with clients and ask enough questions to get a competitive advantage.

Once you are there, your opportunity is to create clients who create clients. Get more ideal clients who can be potential allies, helping you multiply your exposure to people just like them.

This is how you create a career that has longevity, provides you with fulfillment financially, emotionally, psychologically, and most of all, improves your quality of life.

Your branding will help you earn a reputation for providing high value. Create buzz or word of mouth and attract people to you!

Your value will just improve as years go by. Therefore, I am asking you to think long term. As a sales professional, sometimes, we get stuck on short-term thinking because oftentimes, we start from zero every month and we are doing everything we can to hit our immediate sales goals.

Being short sighted is a detriment. You must look at the big picture in the long term and see what you can do to grow your influence and your value at the same time. Do this so you can enjoy the fruits of your labor and not have to worry about chasing a commission check every month.

People frown on salespeople who boast about the value they provide. People believe the same claims when they come from a third party. Ideal clients who become referral partners are the third parties you desperately need.

When you are successful in building your network of ideal clients, you can begin to identify which of them would make good referral partners. The relationships you are building and nurturing will stay with you your entire career. Many will become friends and associates for your lifetime.

And depending on what industry you are in, you will find yourself doing business with your clients' families, their business associates, and colleagues. Your best clients would have it no other way than to have you serve their constituents at same elevated level that you have served them.

Your motivation will always be to do your best to serve your clients. One of the benefits of being indispensable to your niche of clients is found in the law of reciprocity. People will naturally want to return the favor you have bestowed upon them. Your clients will be grateful, so they will want to spread the word about the value you provide. You can help them help you by teaching them how they can help you, which is by connecting you with others who would enjoy how you do business. Make it clear that you serve them at an elevated level by being exclusive.

You do not use time-intensive marketing and prospecting tactics and prefer word of mouth and formal introductions to like-minded individuals.

You have endeared yourself to this audience; they want you to continue to serve them and only need to be informed of what you need and how they can support you. But it is more than that; your clients have colleagues, friends and family who would be just as appreciative of your approach to solving problems. Your clients need to be advised of how you grow your business, and they need you to point out how you can help their circle of influence.

The benefit to you personally is statistically; we already know that referrals are less likely to shop around. They are willing to pay a premium because they know they are getting premium service. The sales cycle is shorter because most of your work is done in advance by your clients who are making the referral. You get to skip rapport building and you are given the trust that you earned from your ideal clients who could pass their trust along to their peers where you benefit tremendously. A secondary benefit to leveraging your satisfied clients is that people frown on salespeople who boast about the value they provide. Prospects are very skeptical.

However, when a third party (Your existing client) gives you praise and acknowledges the value you provide, 84% of referred prospects believe what they are being told. That is huge. Your life becomes easier because you do not have to do the manual grunt work, prospecting inferior quality lists provided by sales managers. The purpose of this book is to get you to be a SYNER, a synergistic sales and marketing professional. Referral Marketing is the foundation for the SYNER.

CHAPTER 05

GOALS ON PURPOSE— YOUR REASON WHY

The ultimate reason for setting goals is to entice you to become the person it takes to achieve them. There really is a tremendous opportunity in sales, and now as a synergistic sales and marketing professional, you are improving your chances of being a highly paid professional.

As a financial advisor, I have sold investment products to doctors, family practitioners and that sort, and was surprised to see that our earnings were similar. As a financial advisor, I had a lot less education than the doctor with similar earnings.

I also know doctors who are surgeons and specialists that make a lot more than the general practitioner in family practice and more than I was making at that time. The point is that sometimes people do not know their value. I want you to take your work seriously and see the opportunity you have in front of you.

You have an opportunity to raise your game by setting goals that are high— BHAG (Big Hairy Ass Goals) are goals that scare you! Stretch yourself, do not underestimate yourself.

You may exceed all your expectations. How do you get there? By doing a lot of little things right. How do you eat an elephant? One bite at a time.

Understand that selling is one of the highest paid professions. And if you work smart, it can be rewarding on several levels, not just financial.

What is even more exciting is that, if you work smart, you work more efficiently and less becomes more.

When you are enthusiastic about what you do and you are enthusiastic about your clients, you are excited about the solutions you provide.

When you function as an advocate for your clients, you might not fit in to some selling cultures where pressure selling is the norm. Not every organization will see the long-term benefits of this value-added approach to selling.

The conflict is ingrained in some companies and or industries. I am not going to go into the details about careers you should avoid, you can figure that out on your own.

When you look at your SWOT analysis, you are going to learn which products and which industries fit your personality. You should work within your preferred product categories. When you do, you increase your chances for success.

Do not make the mistake of chasing money per se; an easy mistake to make is to look for the profession in selling that pays the most because it is a hot trend.

New industries are great if you are excited you can make things happen fast. However, if you do not really connect with the product or how it serves people, do not grasp the product's benefits. It is going to be frustrating for you, and so my recommendation is, be sure to align yourself properly.

When selecting a selling situation, evaluate all the important areas starting with the product, industry, and your personality. Once you get started, quickly identify ideal clients, and set lofty goals for yourself using my goal attainment method. Use the strategies that have been given to you to reach those goals.

Make a commitment to yourself; once you have made the decision on the market and product, allow yourself time to learn what works and what does not work with your presentation, and then begin referral marketing.

You may never be perfect, and you will never reach perfection, but if you give up too soon, you will never gain from the lessons you have learned. Again, documenting your experience every step of the way helps you identify where you can tweak your process, so use customer relationship software or CRM of your choice right away. Look for patterns and do your best to interpret the data and trends in your own experience.

You are going to succeed by climbing the ladder, and each rung on that ladder will be a lesson that you learned through trial and error. You are a detective at this stage, your objective is to constantly improve.

Proper goal setting will keep you motivated. When you are tied to something that is purposeful, you become a man on a mission. I am not a religious person but by setting goals that are highly personal and are connected to people you love; your whole life takes on new meaning.

There's tremendous power in having a strong reason to do what you do! Often, this is the missing piece. Daily affirmations which include your reason you are in business will keep you going. Simply reciting why you are making the effort to be an indispensable servant leader will help drive you to new heights.

When you set your goals, make sure you are setting them in a way that aligns them with all the personal attributes you will learn in this chapter. You will be learning how to be true to yourself, and your authenticity is going to be enormously powerful when you sell.

People can tell when you are sin. e and when you're looking out for their best interests; and that's very powerful.

Authenticity is a major part of what this book is all about. In the process, you will be performing in ways salespeople are not known for.

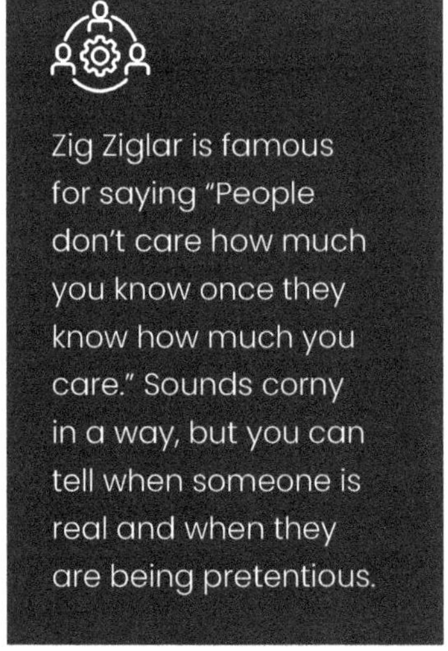

I once watched the 'Family Feud' when the survey question being asked was, "What are the least trusted professions?" (Where people do not trust or something along those lines), and the obvious number one answer was lawyer. But you know, salesman came in the top two or three followed by politicians. The survey did not differentiate between car salesman, or solar salespeople, etc. just salespeople. So differentiating yourself as a servant leader, establishing yourself as a trusted advisor, and referral marketing will be to your advantage. Knowing your reason applies to product, company, and your marketing approach, and this can be powerful.

In this chapter, we will expand on the value of being a trusted advisor in any industry, and how you can improve your motivation.

You are about to learn how to tap into the same kind of power you are building for converting clients and reflect on your own increased personal power.

Where would we be if we were only concerned with bettering our fellow man or ideal clients without creating a life that we love at the same time? You will be able to create great client experiences and improve your experience at the same time.

We can apply the same dynamic process we used to discover how to best serve our clients at the highest level and do the same for ourselves.

Typically, goal setting experts suggest that you have goals and work towards your goals. Then there are smart goals—goal experts promote breaking your goals down into small sections so that you can work on them incrementally to achieve them.

Another approach is to create a vision board; an album of photos made into collage to keep your goals in plain view by placing the collage on a wall where you can see it every day.

However, not many people teach which goals are worthy or the most powerful to help fuel your passion and pull you through the rungs on the ladder. How do you pick the goals that move you the most?

I once read a statement saying lots of people can tell you how to reach your goals, but few if any helps you choose the right goals.

I will say this, my thinking may not be universal, but for me and for a lot of people who are thinking like the platinum rule suggests, which simply says treat people the way they want to be treated. You have more power when you choose goals that move you for deeply personal reasons.

Unfortunately, many of us need to take a closer look at ourselves and identify what our motivations are and rank them in terms of power. You may have come across some critical information when you did your SWOT analysis.

While looking at your strong points in your analysis, you may have discovered a connection between your strongest skill sets and the things that you like to do. Certainly, making the connection between your best skills and how they translate into value for your clients is powerful.

Most people have goals that are materialistic in nature, and when you look at what the motivation is behind their goals, usually it is because they bought into chasing material items that represent status.

Typically, cars and houses are targeted. Usually, those types of goals are constructed not to satisfy the individual, but to keep up with the Joneses. These goals are a way of communicating to the world that you are successful.

I did a personal study on the top regrets people have just before dying, and nothing "material" was on that list. Could we be misguided when it comes to what has real value in our lives?

What shows up in the research of people's wishes before dying typically has to do with not following their dreams, not taking risks, not using their God given talent, and not spending more time with the people they love.

We are going to zero in on high value in terms of our goals, because being a person of high integrity pays a huge dividend in our lives. The conscientious salesman operates on a different level.

Interestingly, people who were about to lose their lives felt the most important thing they owned were their memories with friends and family.

People make the world go round, but most of us spend most of our time trying to isolate ourselves from others until we wake up and realize our greatest assets are our family and friends.

There is value in telling people in your life that they are important to you, how you feel about them, expressing love, spending time with family and so forth. They need to hear it.

You have a tremendous opportunity to use what you are learning here about relationship capital management and set more meaningful goals. An example of this sort of powerful goal setting would be to find a way to be a servant leader to members of your family by providing the same gentle touch that I am suggesting you perform with your ideal clients.

Material goals may still be your objective, but now you can look at them through a new lens. Look at the people closest to you in your life and ask yourself, how nice would it be if I could add value to their lives?

We all have challenges, and we all need help, we just do not ask for help as much as we should. We are a community, yet we strive to be independent until it hurts. Then we finally realize that our friends and family are all that really matters.

Open your eyes and your heart and ask, who are the people in my circle who are less fortunate than I who I could commit to helping through my newly found success as a SYNER?

Use their struggle as a motivator for you. Make the struggles your people are experiencing part of your experience and your goal setting.

My hope is that by adding more gravity to your goals and more emotion, you will become more efficient as a salesperson, working with a purpose bigger than yourself.

Consider how your newly acquired wealth can change a loved one's life. Think college education for a nephew, down payments for first homes for younger family members, health insurance or long-term care for the elderly, your favorite charities, themed family vacations, medical procedures, dental or orthodontist services, tutors, therapists, drug rehabilitation, etc.

It may work out that a new house or car may still be your target for yourself and family, but this approach will change how you look at materialism. You will grow, and when you satisfy your basic needs, there will be tremendous power in helping others. Be conscientious and use this power!

Your continually growing ability to develop and manage your relationship capital will create more quality time in your life, allow you to get more done in less time, and you will be able to do more financially for the people that are important in your life.

My assertion for adding more power when setting a goal is; when you set goals, imagine yourself hitting your financial goals and being able to do things that bring joy to the people in your inner circle, whether it is your parents, your children, struggling relatives, grandparents, etc.

At the end of the day, these are the people who are the most important in your life; you do not want to wait until it is too late to create memories. You are working in one of the highest paid professions; you need leverage at every step to keep you motivated and focused.

Setting goals with a powerful purpose gives you another advantage. When you get up every day, you will naturally remind yourself why you work so hard and maintain your momentum. At the end of your time on earth, you do not want to look back with a handful of regrets.

Jokingly I heard someone once say that they have never seen a U-Haul following a hearse. You can still achieve material wealth. You can also make a shift to putting value into the lives of family members and friends. Or it may be more moving to support the charities important in your life. When you put your goals together in this way, you are giving your goals more importance and improving the odds of hitting them.

Your experience will create something hard to come by for some people, and that's pure happiness! Being happy is the goal. Servant leadership provides tremendous value to your clients.

Making the people in your life happy by sharing your wealth and creating happiness in their lives also creates joy and happiness in your life. The memories you will be creating and the feelings of appreciation you will receive cannot be bought.

At the end of the day, when you make someone else happy, you cannot help but get some of that happiness on yourself; it just permeates your body when you bring joy to other people.

When you set your goals, set them with a plan on how you can serve humanity in mind, and you will be an unstoppable force.

To help you tap into the power of goal setting, break your goals down into five categories: career, financial, personal growth, relationships, spiritual and health.

Those are the five categories that I think are most important. Number one: your career goals—ask yourself where you will be in five years. Do you see yourself being a business owner? Do you see yourself continuing to expand your existing business? It is up to you, but if you do not have a target to aim at, then you are going to drift.

Second on the list are financial goals. What are you going to do with your earnings? Are you going to buy a home? Build an investment portfolio for retirement? Take care of an elderly parent?

Once again, figure out the parts of your life you want to develop. Areas that if you were to recognize their importance to your overall happiness and address them, you would see how they may help you with motivation.

The third goal setting opportunity is in your own personal development. We all need to continue to grow to remain relevant.

You can only maintain your value by furthering your expertise. This means obtaining an additional degree, expanding your knowledge through reading, etc. There are a lot of different methods you can use in identifying how you can grow personally. Your SWOT Analysis is an excellent tool to help identify areas of opportunity. Continuing to increase your depth of knowledge and expertise can be another powerful source of motivation.

The third key area in goal setting is setting Relationship Goals. Look at the people who are most important in your life. Should you be investing more quality time with certain friends or family members? It takes a friend to be a friend, and staying in touch is important. Someone must keep the relationships strong. You are a developing leader and should want to be the person to make the calls and send the cards.

Are there people in your family who are struggling? The family members who need and deserve the help would never ask.

You may be in position to help, but you just have not made time to ask. What about the children in your family, how could you be more supportive? Look for members of your family who have specific challenges that up until now, you did not see as an opportunity for you to help.

The fifth goal to help you enjoy a balanced life are health and spirit goals. We must make it a point to take care of our bodies and minds. We have nothing without our physical and mental health; therefore, we all need to maintain our bodies and our attitudes. Your attitude will determine your altitude. Carve out time for recreation and rest. If you do not have a religion or spiritual practice, find something to help you with your inner peace.

PART 03

At this point, you have taken a deep look inside yourself and you are figuring out answers to the most important questions that will drive your success.

Your power lies in knowing why you are positioning yourself in a certain way, who you will be serving, and who will be included in your support group.

Through goal setting, you have figured out how to tap into goals with a purpose. You have loved ones you will support and give them a better life. You are setting yourself up to have strong relationships, both professionally and personally once you figure out your 'reason why.'

Your opportunity now is to learn how to sustain your momentum and jump the hurdles you undoubtedly will face.

So how are you going to manage your motivation? As you go through these exercises you have been shown in this text, your motivation is going to be high, you will feel strong, but you must learn how to maintain it.

Maintaining your motivation is a challenge for most of us. I would like to share with you some ideas on how you can stay motivated.

There is another benefit to having purposeful goals; instead of having to push yourself, you become pulled in, gaining momentum by the gravity of your purpose.

You still want to write your goals down, break them down into small pieces and make them specific, measurable, achievable, realistic, and time-bound— tied to a deadline.

We have been introspective and have solid evidence for why we can achieve our goals, and why we feel that we are deserving of the rewards.

To help you get there, you must step into a future version of yourself. My intention is to get you to see your value and the value you create, leveraging relationship capital. If you can see yourself being a servant leader, you naturally have a vision of yourself serving at a high level.

My hope is that you see yourself succeeding using what I am teaching you. When you are properly aligned with your talent and values, you are more likely to fight through the challenges you face in the beginning.

Even with the best laid out plans, you must be willing to fight through your own ignorance. Everyone makes mistakes when they start out. In fact, these mistakes are important, but moving past your mistakes is a requirement.

Your early mistakes are your Rites of Passage. Your confidence will be birthed by your ability to learn quickly from your mistakes. If you can find a way to laugh at yourself in the process, you will blow through this phase.

Do not forget that confidence is what you are selling in every case, and the only way to have authentic confidence is to be competent.

You can learn from the mistakes people make, either through personal experience or the experience of others. You will be championing your personal cause identified in the goal making process. A champion is not defined by winning. A champion is defined by continually picking himself up. Always advance forward!

If you lack confidence in the beginning, you can improve by taking good notes on everything you learn. If you need to work on your self-image, my recommendation is that you start out by doing mirror work.

Mirror work starts by writing down descriptions of your ideal self. Give yourself permission to grow into your ideal persona. Now put together a power talk. You are going to step outside of yourself and look yourself in the eyes and tell yourself what you are going to do to become the Badass you see on the horizon.

You might tell yourself I'm going to be the top guy in his company, I'm aiming on being one of the best in this industry, no one serves clients better than I do, no one works harder than I, no one knows this product better than I do; then do what it takes to get there.

Now recite this power talk in your mirror until you own this vision. In the beginning, you may feel silly standing in front of that mirror delivering your power talk. You can eliminate the silly feeling by working on your goals every day and always ending your day on a positive vibe. Eventually, there will be nothing silly about it. You will know your mission, know what you must do and how to do it, which means you are in motion. You need motion to sustain motivation.

Continue to tell yourself what you are aiming at; you are going to make those statements a reality. I suggest you do this exercise every day and look yourself in the eyes. People tend to be telling the truth when they can look you in the eyes. You will be looking into your own eyes. Remember the worst lie you could ever tell is the lie you tell yourself. You are creating your future truth.

When you recite these affirmations and look yourself in the eyes, you are not going to want to let yourself down. At your core, you are going to want to move into the vision you have created for yourself.

Work at it a little bit every day. And I do mean a little bit when you start, because sometimes if your expectations are too high for any given day, you run the risk of not continuing the following day. You are building your personal vision, so it is more important to take some action than no action at all.

Effectively managing your energy is how you prevent yourself from going into slumps and losing your momentum. Allow yourself to fail, allow yourself to do small things some days, large things other days. Another recommendation I have is, when you see small amounts of transformation, you celebrate! Choose how you plan to celebrate but be sure to pick something that is personal to you.

For me, it is a glass of wine, sometimes, I watch television. You pick your poison, pick your reward, but you must celebrate. I like to end each day by being able to say I made at least one critical move or made a critical decision.

I will find something that I can be proud of. Ideally, you want to do something every day that is massive, and it does not have to be dropping a bomb.

It could just mean that you have made a decision that improves your approach—that is massive, you just made your whole approach different; that is important. A decision like that can be made in an instance, but that is important.

Make sure you see each of your triumphs clearly and continue to do the daily work. I am going to cite Zig Ziglar the motivational speaker. I saw him in person a few times (rest in peace) and honestly, I did not resonate with him at first. But I learned to appreciate him more and more as I progressed in my career.

One of the funniest things he ever said to me, which was the most valuable, was a story told about someone who told him that motivation does not last. His response was, neither does bathing, which is why we recommend it daily.

I am messing that up, but the idea is, you must work on your attitude every day just like you must maintain the health of your teeth by brushing daily. Motivation should be included in your daily routine, and you can start off in the mirror every day.

One of the celebrities I follow, "Idris Elba," has a routine. Every morning when he wakes up, he sits at the side of his bed. I do not know if he sits for 5 or 10 minutes, but he just does not move. He just sits there and clears his head before he even lets his feet touch the ground. I tried that and I like the results.

Some people meditate, and others exercise to get their mind and body invigorated.

Others may do any combination of routines to start their day on the right track. Depending on your situation, you may use one routine heavily to get on track then change as you progress. The idea is to get you to be an active participant in your experience, otherwise random thinking and loose priorities will take you over.

I am suggesting you create a routine to start each day from the very start and make it easy for yourself. You want to be authentic and aligned with who you are as an individual. It may take a while to figure out what works best for you. Do not fall into the trap of listening to too many people giving you advice. You just want the general idea and understand that you are getting ideas and innovating for what works best for you.

CHAPTER 06

THE PLATINUM RULE—
HOW TO CHANGE THE GAME

You have identified your ideal client. You are developing your brand and professional identity, and you are setting your goals for how you will serve your ideal clients and other VIPs in your experience. You are now on your way to being a standout performer in your niche, in your company, and potentially, in your industry.

You are setting yourself apart. When you put your personality out front, you eliminate competition because you will be unique. No one will resemble you because of the stance you are adopting for how you characterize yourself, who you choose to serve, and the service you are creating for those who will be in your circle.

This is a game changer. Most people have heard of the Golden Rule. The Golden Rule is biblical. It is simply states, "Do unto others as you would have them do unto you." You are going to do better than the golden Rule. Do unto others as you want others to do unto you sounds good, but you will do much better than that.

Golden Rule Versus Platinum Rule

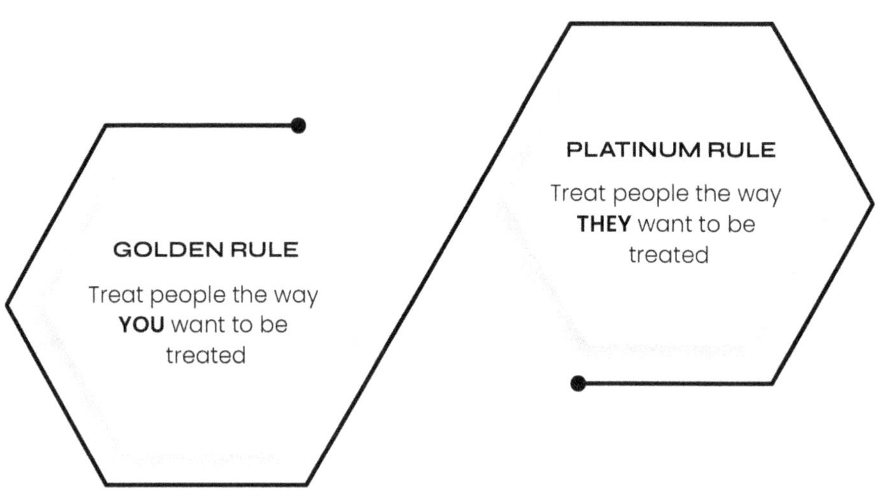

As a synergistic sales and marketer, you are a SYNER, not in the biblical sense of course. Your focus is going to be on your client. Treating them like you treat yourself is not good enough. You will treat them the way they want to be treated. You have your preferences, your likes, and your motivations, assuming your clients have the same preferences and motivations that you have is a misstep.

The better approach is using The Platinum Rule.

The Platinum Rule Is when you treat your clients exactly the way they want and need to be treated. That is a departure from The Golden Rule.

You will be serving at a higher level, and that is what differentiates you from your competition. This is what makes you the go to guy. The Golden Rule is flawed, we can do better than that. You are going to go one step beyond. You want to practice empathy. You really want to do what you can to feel what it is like to wear another person's shoes. You want to know as much as you can about your client. You want to create a dossier. Your cost for doing so is to keep good records and manage communications effectively.

As a servant leader, you must become good at customer relationship management. You are going to want to use software to keep track of all the information you collect from your clients and track all sales and marketing activities that you perform with your clients.

You are going to continuously receive and solicit feedback form your clients. You, in turn, will be their caretaker or fiduciary and you are going to support them in ways that you have never imagined. This goes beyond being a product provider. You are going to pay attention to problems your clients are experiencing and problems you anticipate in the future.

When you can do that, you are going to help them solve these problems, even if it is not with your product. You are going to always keep your eyes open looking for opportunities to help your clients, whether you earn a commission or not.

You are going to be talking to people in your niche often, and when you are presented with an opportunity to help someone, you do.

You may help just by connecting people; putting people together who may never have met if it were not for you. People who could help each other. You end up being a broker of change.

You find opportunities like this more often when you are looking for them!

You are building a reputation as a trusted advisor, someone that should be involved in major decisions. Done correctly, you might find yourself invited to important staff meetings and given the opportunity to provide insight.

The knowledge you acquire being an initiative-taking problem solver will serve you in many ways. When you hear of opportunities in your everyday activities that are suitable for sharing with your ideal clients, you do so.

When you position yourself as a servant leader, your clients will be loyal. They will not do business with anyone else, except with you. And that is what you want.

To make the most of The Platinum Rule, you want to be aware of personality differences. In the next chapter, you will learn more about identifying personality differences. Knowing how to recognize and how to best communicate with people who do not share your communication style helps you expand your influence.

In your role as trusted advisor, you will focus on integrity. Always tell the truth, no matter how bad it hurts. You want to be the person your clients can depend on.

Give it to him straight. One mistake salespeople make is that they patronize their clients. They tell them what they think their clients want to hear. That is a big mistake. A study done by a Washington D.C. Think tank discovered during a recession, that salespeople who were able to sell steadily had a common characteristic. This productive group of salespeople challenged their clients and were able to provide stern advice and make sales when many clients were content with sitting on the fence until the economy improved. Fewer salespeople are productive during a down market.

The difference was that they were not afraid to tell their clients the truth. These salespeople were very persuasive telling clients that you have trusted me during good times, and you need to trust me during bad times. I have the solution to your problems right now, this is what I suggest you do. People want leadership, even more so when they are in trouble. Can you see how servitude leads to leadership?

Depending on your product, company, and your industry, you might find yourself in a position to help your clients make critical decisions. And if you establish a history of being forthright, you become someone on whom they can rely.

People want to buy from people they trust. On the opposite spectrum, if you make a mistake, you need to own that mistake and fix it. You need to fix it with vigor. Again, having made a mistake and managing it properly increases your credibility and your trust factor.

Everyone makes mistakes, it is how you respond to these matters that sets you apart from the rest. There will be occasions when your product does not solve your client's problems.

When you do not have the solution but know how to solve the problem by recommending a competitor who can solve the problem, do so.

However, make sure whoever you recommend is on the same page as you. Make sure you know exactly how your referrals will be managed, and that they will return the favor. You cannot always have all the answers. But you might know of another way to solve the problem, not using your product solution.

And when you sell away from your own product line, unless you are contractually forbidden to do so, you make sure that competitor is on your team. Let them know that you expect him to return the favor. You keep track of all your communications with this competitor in your CRM software and make him a part of your referral partner team.

Once you have established yourself as an indispensable resource to your ideal clients (by the way, you do not have to go through a recession), you have earned the right to ask for referral opportunities. Set the stage by advising your ideal clients that you afford yourself the time to address client needs by including them in your business development.

Let us just face it, running ads, cold calling and cold email are time and cost intensive. If you had to build your business using those tactics, you would have to reduce the attention and services you give your ideal clients.

You need to continue to bring new clients into your business to accomplish business growth and stellar service simultaneously; and you are going to need help.

You need support to continually bring more ideal clients into your mix and not spend unnecessary time with potential clients that do not fit your ideal client profile.

Cold business may be less profitable, not so easy to work with because there will not be much trust at the outset. Non-referred business will shop around because they have no loyalty and become ghosts when another seller gets into their head.

You know the value of having strong relationships, but it is likely you are not capitalizing on the leverage you have when you develop these relationships and optimize your business.

Let us talk referral marketing. Referral marketing is the foundation for the synergistic sales and marketing professional. There are multitudes of marketing tactics, but referral marketing is the number one tactic for the SYNER.

The strategy is to first provide superior service delivered only to your ideal clients.

When you already have a few ideal clients and have a reputation for being an indispensable resource, you can build on these relationships in a mutually beneficial way. These people, these clients, are going to be your resource for more clients like themselves.

Ideally, you want clients who bring you more clients. Some of them will refer to you naturally without being asked. However, they may not know exactly what your criteria is for identifying ideal clients for you. Your obligation, your responsibility, is to help them understand how you work best.

Share your story for how you focus on quality service afforded by client support. The less time you spend on crude sales prospecting and marketing tactics, the more time you can work on your client's behalf. Let them know this is your secret.

You want to do more than just say I want more clients like you. Let them know the attributes of your business relationship you want to replicate, their buying behavior or usage, their posture with you, the business size that allows you to do your best work. Paint a clear picture and then ask them to introduce you to more people of this type.

The difference between initiative-taking referral marketing and reactive referral marketing is that you are establishing criteria, and you are being active in soliciting exactly what you want.

Your perceived value to your ideal clients should be high when you are a servant leader; utilize the platinum rule while serving your clients. Your clients will be happy to introduce you because you are an asset to them. When they refer you to their colleagues, they know they are doing their colleagues a favor and building goodwill.

You explain how when you get referrals to individuals or companies that do not fit your criteria, you are taking valuable time away from what you do best.

So it is crucial that you have a clear understanding of what you want, and in turn, communicate these criteria to your ideal clients. Once you have accomplished the explanation, you want to take it a step further and explain to them, or I should say, teach them how to represent you properly.

You accomplish this by teaching your ideal clients how to sell you and providing them with point of sell materials. You can create cheat sheets, check lists, qualifying questions, and anything you discover that will help them help you.

You could also provide common or frequently asked questions and answers to support their efforts. You might even want to take it a step further and create a script for your ideal clients to use with people they refer to you.

Typically, 20% of your business will be made up of ideal clients. These are the clients you want to invest most of your time in. Some of these ideal clients will be ideal referral partners for you. It will be these clients you want to enlist support.

When you take that 20% and you dive deeper, 4% of that group will be the cream of the crop. You want to make special notice of these people. These clients are the ultimate clients for you.

Actively identifying who these people are and how to gain access to more of them makes up for the fact you are going to be dealing with fewer people. If you are typical, 80% of your business is going to come from these ultimate clients.

The top 4% of your clients are your heavy hitters. You want more of these, but they are the exception, not the rule. You are on your way when you start to develop a reputation for having such integrity. You will start to attract more ideal clients as you continue. Ideal clients want ideal vendors, so do not give up your focus on quality vs quantity. You cannot serve or advise everyone and when you specialize in serving a specific group of people, you begin to know their unique challenges and how to best serve them. You are earning their respect and should not be surprised when clients include you in major decisions. The law of reciprocity will work in your favor when clients are motivated to help you because of how you have helped them. Sometimes, you may even be sought after and attract new business because you will be noticed just because of how you conduct business.

So congratulations! You have taken the first step in creating your referral partner network. The idea is to continue to build your network and have your network do the heavy lifting for your business. In the beginning, things might be slow in developing. However, be patient it is worth the effort and time spent focusing on these key concepts.

PERSONALITY SELLING

PART 01

In this chapter, we will talk to you about how to maximize The Platinum Rule by becoming familiar with personality differences.

Every individual is unique. In learning to brand yourself, you built on your uniqueness to build your brand and set yourself apart. Your uniqueness is what eliminates your competition because there is only one you. Being the best version of yourself is your competitive advantage.

Conversely, recognizing the personality differences of your clients can strengthen your rapport and improve your effectiveness in your efforts to serve their needs.

Hippocrates, the Greek physician, is the individual who first produced personality theory. Hippocrates's model included four personality groupings. Contemporary social scientists have expanded Hippocrates's personality theory.

The popular Myers Briggs personality type test is built on the foundation that was established by Hippocrates. Myers Briggs has 16 different personality types identified.

Personality typing has been accomplished in a myriad of ways. The Enneagram has labeled 9 personalities.

There are several authors who have published different labels and simplified tests to identify the most common personality traits using the four main personalities groups. Hippocrates's four labels included the sanguine, choleric, melancholic, and phlegmatic.

Some of the tests you find online use animals as metaphors to represent a given personality, and others use colors. The personality testing system I first encountered, which seems to be the most user friendly for sales professionals uses 4 descriptive labels, best suited for our use.

I have used the following simple personality labeling system successfully with my own clients and with my employees. I have turned salespeople's careers around, helping them identify personality differences and communicate more effectively. Results can be immediate when salespeople become more in tune with the unique attributes of individual personalities. They will become more effective communicators and make more connections and more sales.

DRIVER 

- Bottom line focused
- Impatient
- Wants answers yesterday
- Best handled by being direct

EXPRESSIVE 

- Talkative
- Keep an agenda allow some time for small talk but stick to the plan

ANALYTICAL 

- Loves information
- Tendency to drown in information overload
- Best way to satisfy is to have conclusions backed up by deductive reasoning

AMIABLE 

- Very easy to commit
- Great listeners
- Make sure all influencers are considered when making agreements

I believe that if you can make personality theory as simple as possible, you will be able to use the theory consistently. If you overcomplicate personality typing, attempting to recognize every nuance people possess, you start getting into the weeds and get lost in the forest.

When you start getting into the labels that Myers Briggs uses for example, you will become remarkably familiar with your own personality. However, after that, you will be at a loss trying to figure out the personality attributes of all 16 Myers Briggs personality types. You may have experience with a given personality typing system, hence, you are encouraged to use with whatever you are comfortable. I too subscribe to the Platinum Rule and suggest you use the system you are familiar with if you have prior experience doing so.

It is up to you. If you want, you can go online and take a personality test of your choice and zero in on your own personal attributes and use labels that resonate with you. I encourage you to become familiar with one of the simpler versions for practical purposes. Online, you will find both free and paid versions of personality type tests with detailed explanations of their differences.

I am not going to provide a personality test as a part of this book, but what I am going to do is help you identify the four basic labels and their traits I have used successfully. Armed with personality type, you will improve your ability to communicate effectively with people and in the long run, improve your ability to sell.

The Platinum Rule is more easily accomplished in your communication with your client when you can identify individual personalities and their preferences for how they want to be addressed—this is a tremendous advantage.

The platinum rule simply states that you want to treat people the way they want to be treated. Understanding personality type helps you understand that individuals speak different languages depending on their personality. You and your clients may both be speaking English; however, different styles of communication can change the meaning of what you are trying to communicate.

Most of communication comes from non-verbal communication; how you say what you say versus what you say. Rather than go into an extensive explanation of how to manage non-verbal communication, I contend that if your intentions are noble and you follow The Platinum Rule, your non-verbal communication will fall in line with your verbal communication.

Cultural dimensions of communication also play a role, and again, I contend that learning basic personality typing and utilizing the Platinum Rule will resolve

---

potential issues with communicating across race and cultures. Your advantage will be that you will be able to adapt to the personality in front of you.

Some personalities require that you give more details. Others really do not want to have expansive explanations; they want bottom line information. The Platinum Rule suggests that when you identify a tendency, you appease the given personality with strategic communication.

 I do not want you to think that you are pandering to people based on what your client's personalities are. What you are doing is catering to them, there is a difference. You want people to feel they are in good hands. People buy from people they trust, and they buy from people they like. When you speak to people in ways, they are accustomed to speaking your ability to build rapport increases dramatically.

So it is not pandering, it is being smart, it is improving the accuracy of your communication. Imagine if you knew that your client's preferred language is Spanish, and you also speak Spanish, but you insist on speaking English. If you are bilingual and know that their preference is to speak in Spanish, would you speak English with them? No, you would speak Spanish; and that is an advantage because you can use words with which they are familiar.

Even though they speak decent English, by being able to switch to their native language, your chances of accomplishing meaningful agreements and establishing a lasting relationship goes through the roof.

Learning different personality types and communication styles acknowledges that everybody speaks a different language even when their primary language is English.

When you can identify the way people are accustomed to communicating, you will naturally start speaking their language, use the timing, duration, and frequency of communication they prefer.

You bring yourself closer to having a working relationship when you can communicate effectively. That is what personality selling is; it is knowing that you have a unique personality and that you communicate best when you are talking to someone that shares your style. But when you know the Platinum Rule and you understand personality differences, you can cater to individuals who are different from you and will still be successful.

PART 02

Let us take a deep dive into the personality type model I think is the easiest to understand and put it into practice. People use a variety of models like I mentioned before. I do not know who the originator is of the four labels that I am going to use here, so I am not going to give credit.

I have seen several authors use this approach. The four personality types are as follows: The first one is the Amiable, followed by the Expressive, Analytical, and lastly, the Driver.

The Amiable personality represents the smallest group of people you will encounter. Amiable personalities are characterized by people who are very receptive to being sold. They tend to do exactly what you suggest.

Physically, they might resemble your favorite grandmother or aunt. Amiable personalities do not typically have many objections; they trust you right away. Unfortunately, they become victimized by people who are unscrupulous. They are usually protected by another personality type. In a selling situation, they are rare. When you do have the opportunity to serve an amiable personality type, it is surprising how they follow every piece of advice you give without hesitation.

You will love talking with the Amiable client. I want to stress that you should not expect to develop a tremendous number of duplicate Amiable clients. They are just exceedingly rare.

One caution when selling to this personality type; I have had situations where an Amiable person made a large purchase with no questions, just an easy transaction. What often happens is, an amiable individual will have a relative or an attorney or someone who gets involved afterwards.

This third party (person) will often make you unravel everything you have done. Later in this chapter, I am going to speak more about selling someone with this personality type. I will help you put these personalities into the proper perspective by encouraging you to watch a few syndicated episodes of Star Trek. The Star Trek amiable personality is portrayed as Pavel Chekov.

The second personality is the Expressive personality. The Expressive is someone who has the gift of gab. You must be careful because if you are not, you will never get a word in; they will tell you their life stories if you let them.

Expressive personality types can be very personable and sometimes exceedingly difficult to sell. You must be mindful of their love for conversation. You know someone like this. Oftentimes, people who have this talent are told that they would be good in sales.

Having the gift of gab in sales can be a curse. You can easily talk yourself out of a sale. It is a myth that having the gift of gab is a prerequisite for sales success. The Star Trek version of this personality type is Dr. McCoy.

The third personality is the Analytical personality. The analytical personality is a researcher. They are typically numbers oriented. They collect information and tend to be shoppers. They are meticulous, and they love exploring all their options. Analytical personalities have lots of questions. They want to think about and read extensive data on any given topic. I compare this personality to the Star Trek personality Dr. Spok.

The last personality type in this personality type model is the Driver. The driver is a very impatient bottom-line individual. This personality will tell you he does not want to spend a lot of time on researching, and does not want to hear your sales presentation, he just wants to know the bottom line! Alpha males are typically identified as being this personality type.

Driver personalities tend to be leaders, sometimes, they are athletic. They tend to be a little pushy and there is an extremely specific way that you want to deal with the Driver individual. The Driver Star Trek character is Captain Kirk.

We have now reviewed the four different personality types. Next, we will go into how you can effectively work with someone whose personality is clearly different from yours.

PART 03

Obviously, personality theory is not an exact science. Everyone is unique, much more unique than most of these personality tests will show you. Most people are strong in one of the four areas. Their secondary personality plays a key role in some situations.

People like me, who take these tests may score balanced between all four personalities. I am rare. Sometimes, I score that way because I have taken so many of these tests. I have also frequently used them with salespeople for training purposes, so I anticipate the questions. But I am an analytical personality. What is important for you to know is that personality typing is a valid tool.

I am providing you with a guide to help you better understand people, and how you can improve your relationships, build goodwill, and improve your business. Personality theory gives you another way to make the Platinum Rule work for you. Here are typical examples of how a sales professional might work with each of the four typical personalities.

One thing I think is important to acknowledge is there are situations where people change their personality styles. For example, under duress someone who is Expressive could turn into their weakest personality trait; and the exact opposite personality becomes a Driver.

The tool is not perfect, but it is dependable in selling situations because whichever personality style that an individual adopts when they are in the buying mode will be consistent.

You just work with what you experience in your interaction. You do not have to look at all the implications of what you learn by dissecting personality attributes.

When you are fortunate enough to have an Amiable person in front of you, which is rare, you have the rare opportunity to quickly qualify them and make a recommendation without much objection.

However, when qualifying them, find out who the other potential decision makers are. Ask them who they share their business with. You want to determine if there is another person you need to sell. Get them involved early unless your client insists there will not be any questions from their supporters.

You simply ask them how they normally buy, and if they get other people involved in the decisions. This is a key step to take if you want your sale to stick. In review, one characteristic people do not like about Amiable personality types is that they tend to make decisions quickly then change their minds because of outside influences. Afterwards, they share their decision with people close to them who may become naysayers. You must know that is a major possibility with this personality type and treat them appropriately.

When you're selling to someone who's Expressive, you may struggle to get a word in edgewise if you allow them to start a conversation. Give them time after you manage the business at hand if you have time. If you lose control of the conversation, you risk appearing rude when you try to get them back on track. The best way to recover if you lose control is to wait for them to take a breath then quickly interrupt and change the subject. If you must cut them off, apologize and let them know you have time constraints. Tell them you must be focused on what their needs are to help them to make decisions.

The best approach is to recognize this personality early. My advice is to use an agenda to control the conversation. Make a checklist and tell them how you are budgeting your time with the agenda. If not, they will change subjects on you and go on tangents unrelated to your discussion. Create an agenda in writing and let them see it. Walk them through each part of the agenda, check off each stage, and make it clear you must budget your time.

The Analytical personalities are often folks who are numbers oriented. They are researchers and engineers. I had a sales office near Silicon Valley. You could tell the Analytical personalities when they walked in the building. They often wore pocket protectors carrying mechanical pencils and often had notebooks in hand. They can be obvious—the visuals can give them away.

Analytical people speak a different language. When listening to their description of their needs, pay attention to the language they use. You want to write down their keywords. You need to pull out a notepad and use thorough qualifying questions and draw logical solutions. Make sure you qualify them well getting all the fine details. Expect to ask more questions than with other personality types. If you cannot do this because of your personality, refer them to someone who can and share the business.

If they speak in numbers, make sure that when you present solutions, you speak in numerical terms; specifically, the ones about which they are concerned. More importantly, make sure you draw logical conclusions leading to your recommendation. You want to be succinct in your logical solution to their problems. You must assure them that you have done your research, so they do not have to and help them understand how you are saving them time. Ideally, you want to sell yourself as an analytical tool for them. You need to be someone who can prevent them from getting lost in the forest.

Otherwise, Analytical personalities will procrastinate, sleep on it, think about it, etc. If you hear any of the stalling tactics I just illustrated, you have lost control of the situation. You can regain control but do your homework so you can avoid this dance.

Their natural tendency is to research everything; they want to make sure that they are not making any sort of technical mistakes.

If you want to prevent them from disappearing and postpone making decisions for weeks or months, you are going to have to demonstrate that you know the numbers.

You want to make sure they understand that they do not have to do the research because you know everything there is to know about their condition, their problem, and the solution.

Analytical people have tendencies to get overwhelmed with data. When you feed them data, you do not want to overfeed them; you want to strategically layout the facts and have a logical conclusion. If an Analytical client respects you, they could easily become an ideal client and referral partner, and you will not have to do a ton of research for the people they refer to you either. You will inherit the trust you earned from your analytical referral partner. The referrals will shop around less and trust you more.

The Driver personality, for some people, is the most difficult because they are bottom line oriented. If you are not careful, they will dictate to you how you should do your job.

They tend to be alpha males and they are likely to tell you that they do not want to hear your sales presentation. "Just give me the bottom line" is their mantra.

They are very recognizable. I have had a lot of success with alpha males; they respect confidence. On more than one occasion, I have met with Driver personalities and their first comments could be interpreted as an insult. I was not insulted. I could have taken their comments personally, and I could have also seen them as racist, but I did neither.

I just let them know that I was a professional and that if they wanted to get what they needed, they would have to allow me to do my due diligence and play by my rules or leave. No one ever left. I was being tested. This personality is impatient, and if you bend to their initial push, they will judge you as someone not worth their time. I have been successful multiple times using equal amounts of vigor in response to the initial push of these personalities and earned their respect; and in one case, became friends outside of the business we conducted together. When they tell you they do not want you to approach them in a certain way and you know you need to do your due diligence, stiffen your spine, and tell them it does not work that way. Let them know that to be sure you are making a proper recommendation, and if they want to succeed at what they are trying to do, they need to heed your advice.

Connect the dots for them and if you have solid reasons why modifying your approach could have negative consequences, put that out there immediately. If they insist on trying to short circuit your process, fire them! When you stand your ground by cutting them loose in a weird way, you earn their respect. They may even change roles and follow your lead once you establish you have confidence.

Driver personalities typically do not like people who are too flexible, they see them as being "wishy washy."

If it sounds like you need to be a chameleon managing personalities, you do. Unless you discover in your SWOT analysis your ideal client and identifying a niche market is dominated by a specific personality type, then your task is easy. In that case, you are only dealing with one personality style. Usually, that is not the case though. Your opportunity is to use all the strategies and tactics you pick up and decide what works best for you!

PART 04

Personality theory is a valid tool for helping improve communications. You just cannot speak to everyone the same way.

People have different frames of references. They have different ways of using words and they often attribute different meanings to the words you use. You do not need to be a mind reader; personality theory helps you see the basic tendencies quickly. When you can acknowledge personality theory and use it to improve your effectiveness, you set yourself apart and add more value. Most people over-complicate communications because they are poor listeners and do not notice other's nuances.

Without personality theory, you would be limited. If you speak in the only way you feel comfortable speaking in because of your personality, you will resonate more readily with your own personality type but struggle with others.

Having a static communication style is not a crime. Static communication limits your effectiveness. Think about how you improve if you recognize people have different preferences and styles and you adapt to their preferred communication style. Why wouldn't you attempt to be more effective in getting your message across? There are so many variables in making effective communications. Being a SYNER who pays attention to both sales and marketing aspects of communication, you benefit from being more astute in reading people.

In America, you have a great diversity of races, ethnicities, and nationalities. Having an awareness of stereotypes about racial and ethnic groups can help you negotiate with even more people.

Avoid talking yourself out of lucrative opportunities by making assumptions about people based on limited experience with their race, ethnicity, or nationality. Making assumptions about people is a big mistake, and that is why it is important that we never minimize efforts to qualify prospects.

The solution is wrapped up in a book written by Don Miguel Ruiz titled *The Four Agreements*. Simply put, in his book, he identifies 4 agreements that we all should make to improve our relationships with all people.

The Four Agreements are 1. Always do your best 2. Never make assumptions 3. Be Impeccable with your word and 4. Take nothing personally. If you live by The Four Agreements and everything else you are learning in this book, you will prevent yourself from putting your foot in your mouth. And avoid discounting the possibility of doing business with people because of your own prejudices.

Your opportunity as a professional is to accurately read people and to put people together accurately based upon your discovery. You do not make assumptions.

You keep very thorough notes about your ideal client's preferences, their styles, and many of the details we have talked about already. You use customer relationship management software. You document your client's priorities, including family member profiles, hobbies, and traditions. Good documentation makes you better qualified to serve all your clients equally.

You want to know the personality and cultural characteristics associated with your clients as much as you want them to know yours. You want them to know exactly where you are coming from. It makes good sense that you have detailed knowledge of your clients as well. Equipped with this knowledge, you will avoid problems and you will be better qualified to see opportunities.

Learn as much as you can about the people in front of you and avoid prejudices and stereotypes. I want to share a quick story from my experience. I was once in downtown, San Francisco, in one of the financial institutions I serviced.

There was a gentleman who was homeless; he looked very dirty even though he did wear a tie, his tie was filthy.

He had an odor, and no one wanted to talk to this man. I sat him down and I qualified him. I learned he was extremely wealthy.

He was not in the best shape mentally, I discovered why. He was in deep mourning over the loss of his spouse. He shut down his normal existence, sold his cars and home and began hoarding money.

He lived in a small hotel on skid row, and he would visit his money once per day and drink the free coffee in the lobby. He had multiple banking relationships I learned, all maxing out his Federal Deposit Insurance. No one wanted to spend much time with this gentleman. I made him comfortable and interviewed him thoroughly and it turned out he easily had a dozen passbooks with 100,000 in each one.

If I adopted the attitude of the others, I would have never established rapport with this gentleman. I would never have earned his trust and who knows where that money would have ended up.

We were able to capture a lot of his investment funds because I took the time to get to know him.

I take full credit for investing his funds because I did not allow myself to use the same filter that other people in our institution used to prejudge him.

This is a potential trap we all can potentially fall into. Because of the way someone dresses, their personal hygiene, race, ethnicity, and culture. Do not fall into this trap by allowing prejudices and stereotypes to influence our thinking.

CHAPTER 08

OPTIMIZING YOUR GOOD WILL

PART 01

The Pareto Principle

The Pareto principle, or 80/20 for short, is another leverage point you want to observe and optimize. Understanding and successfully applying the Pareto Principle to your business goals can take your strategy for success to the next level.

Although there is little scientific analysis that either proves or disproves the 80-20 rule's validity, there is much anecdotal evidence that supports the rule as being essentially valid, if not numerically accurate.

Vilfredo de Pareto was an Italian sociologist and economist who, during his studies, realized that, for many events, roughly 80 % of the effects come from 20 % of the causes. It is an uneven distribution that can be found in countless life and business situations. At its core, the 80-20 rule is about identifying an entity's best assets and using them efficiently to create maximum value. Salespeople in a wide range of businesses have demonstrated success by incorporating the 80-20 rule.

For the sales professional, if 20% of your time produces 80% of your results, you should be more careful how you spend your time. Referral Marketing is the obvious first choice for sales professionals when you look at business development opportunities. If 80 % of your sales come from 20 % of your clients and 80% of your profits comes from 20 % of your products or services, it makes sense to focus on your best clients, products, and strategies to find more clients to provide product solutions for, based on their needs.

Most of us know this rule in part. We have always heard that 20% of the sales force is responsible for 80% of the sales. Most salespeople are trying to get into the top 20%. Those already in the top 20% want to continue to improve and reach the top 20% of this group, which is the top 4%. Then continue to reach the very top and join the top 1% of their peers. Referral marketing using the Pareto principle is how you can get there!

PARETO'S PRINCIPLE

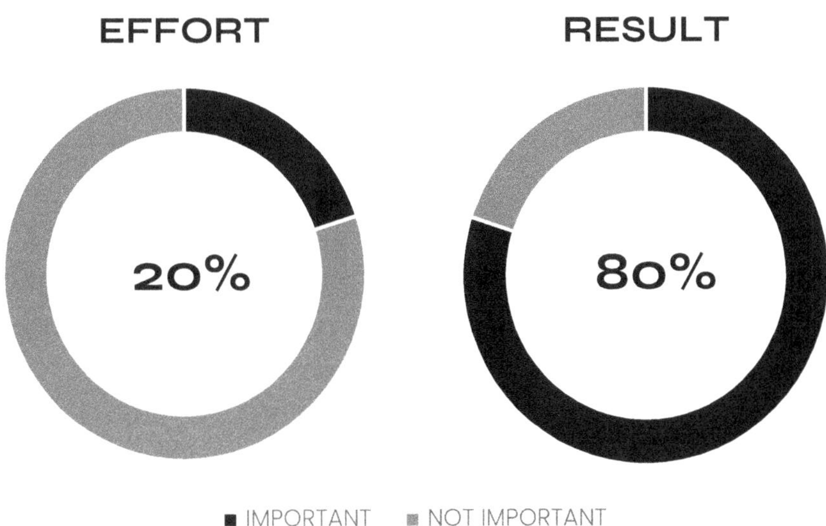

Identifying the characteristics of your customers who represent 80% of your sales will help you find more customers like them and dramatically increase your sales and profits. Your ideal clients are typically going to be the top 20% of your total clients. This is where you want to invest most of your time. You want to nurture and get continual feedback from the clients who are the most valuable to you.

Learn their hot buttons and cater to this group as a servant leader exercising the Platinum Rule. Dissect your top 20 % further, identify the top 4%. The Pareto principle suggests that this group represents 64% of your sales!

Your top 4% is where more than 64% of your sales will come from, which is calculated as 80% of your 80%. Unfortunately, without knowledge of the Pareto principle, this group of clients will go untapped by most sales professionals. Less, really is more, and this is how you work less and make more money by directing your efforts in the right direction.

Invest your time wisely. Not all sales management teams are dialed in to this dynamic and may encourage you to spread yourself around equally among all clients. All I can say is, watch out.

The 80/20 rule is really a fascinating topic. There are two standout books written on the subject; one is written by Perry Marshall titled 80/20 and the other book is "The 80/20 Principle" written by Richard Koch.

Here are proven examples of the Pareto Principle:

➢ 20 percent of the students tend to score grades of 80 percent or greater.

➢ 20 percent of the drivers on the road are responsible for 80 percent of car accidents.

➢ 20 percent of a nation's criminals commit 80 percent of crimes.

➢ 20 percent of employees produce 80 percent of the profit.

It is important to notice that the Pareto Principle is an observation, not a law. Therefore, it does not apply to every single scenario.

Look at your own time management and marketing activities. You can cut back significantly on waste.

Waste is a killer when it comes to any business's bottom line. So the sooner you can identify where you are wasting time and resources, the better.

I want to make sure that you understand how to remove the chaff from the corn. Meaning, a Non SYNER will spend 80% of his time on activities that are time wasters—being busy and being productive are two different things.

Stephen Covey's book "7 Habits of Highly Effective People" is another way the Pareto principle can be expressed. The point is to focus on activities that are yielding the highest return, which are typically activities that engage in strategy and planning the most productive quadrant in Mr. Covey's example.

IMPORTANT

URGENT

NOT URGENT

MANAGE - Firefighting

- Crises Deadline driven projects
- Customer service issues
- Some types of training
- Request for proposals
- Product Issues
- Paperwork

FOCUS - Quality time

- Relationship building
- Identifying Influencers
- Defining your brand
- Building your team
- Testing presentations
- Testing scripts

NOT IMPORTANT

URGENT

NOT URGENT

AVOID - Distractions

- Some phone calls
- Some emails
- Some meetings
- Some reports
- Many Interruptions
- Other's problems

LIMIT - Time wasting

- Social media
- Socializing with sales people
- Long lunches
- TV/Entertainment
- Web browsing
- Junk mail
- Over analysis
- Gossip

Investing your time in activities that are defined as working "on your business" instead of "in your business," are powerful. You are rewarded highly for having strategies like the ones I am teaching you, then testing tactics for their validity in your respective niches.

As soon as you start making money, it is smart to delegate low yielding busy work to an assistant or to a service provider. It will be worth the expense.

You want to make sure that you focus your own energies on activities that give you the highest return on the time you are spending.

In review, 20% of your clients give you 80% of your sales. 20% of these 20% are your ultra-valuable clients. At least potentially, these 4% of clients could account for 64% of your sales. If you have a large enough pool of people to draw from, you can figure out who the 4% and your number 1 client are and provide them with more attention and affect your bottom line in exponential ways.

Double your sales by zeroing in on your best opportunities. Your best customers are your existing customers, recategorize them using the Pareto principle. Getting lots of referrals is not the best strategy, getting the right referrals from the right people is. All referrals are not created equally. Invest your time wisely.

There appears to be a debate as to the effectiveness of making cold calls; I say they still work; the question is are they efficient? If you must make them, stop as soon as you can. The way to escape cold calling is to get referrals from every sale until you can parse your clients and activities, using the Pareto Principle and other tactics you are learning in this book.

Identifying your strong points is the foundation for personal branding and is especially important so that you can match yourself with the right clients, the right products, and the right companies. Knowing your numbers and adjusting your strategy is pure leverage.

You optimize by focusing on your areas of opportunity and how they relate to your specific performance. Part of being an optimist is focusing on opportunities and ignoring the naysayers. Being a realist is knowing your numbers, whether we are talking about choosing referral partners or filtering your entire business. Use 80/20 to reorganize your time and activities to improve your effectiveness.

My Top Twenty Insights Inspired by the Pareto Principle

1. People who employ 80/20 thinking are good at achieving happiness.

2. Effective 80/20 thinkers are experts at prioritizing and delegating the rest.

3. 80/20 thinking supports picking tasks with the highest reward that require the least effort.

4. Life-changing insight requires consistent, high-value thinking and reflection.

5. Focus increases individuality, which is the essence of being a human being.

6. Do more with less, not more with more.

7. Never sacrifice time or love for money.

8. Focus on the value, disregard the waste. Resources that have weak effects should be ignored.

9. Successful people identify value and adapt themselves to the world.

10. Decisions based on superior economics always yield the highest returns.

11. Convert your best talents into economic wealth.

12. Capitalize on the 20% of your personality that differentiates you from your competition to achieve rock-star success.

13. Success is caused by steady application and sudden insight.

14. Develop the facility to mentally block out the bottom 80%.

15. Specialize in something that fills you with enthusiasm and passion.

16. Act less. Action drives out thought, and it is the thought that directs meaningful action.

17. Time management is not the problem. We are awash in time. Time *use* is the problem. Most genius work is done in little time.

18. Achievement is driven by insight and selective action.

19. Outsource everything that is not within your core competencies.

20. Leverage capital (both human and money).

PART 02

Creating Clients Who Create Clients

As a SYNER, cultivating referral partners is your foundation. I suggest starting small when selecting referral partners. Develop the referral partnership carefully. Create just three ideal clients who will serve as referral partners, allow yourself time to maximize your efforts, and leverage your time to maximize referral yield.

These three should be selected from your core ideal clients. Your top 20%. Remember you are building a team of ideal clients you identify as great referral partners. Other great clients may fall short as partners, but you do not have to cancel or neglect the relationship.

Allocate your time or program; accordingly, the idea here is to understand that you are in the relationship capital development phase. So just like a professional sports team, you are developing referral partners out of people who are raw to begin with.

In phase two, you will be focused on relationship capital management. You are going to manage your "A" players, so the goal at this point is to identify three key referral partners before you advance on to any other marketing activities.

As your priority, focus on developing these three A players. Make sure they meet the criteria we spoke about earlier.

You are going to be their caretaker and you do not want to be committed to someone who will not be dependable or who does not grasp what you are trying to accomplish, because this is a relationship and relationship must be on a two-way street, which brings me to the next important fact "motivation."

PART 03

One of the keys to being successful working with referral partners is understanding their motivations. Every individual has different motivations; this is the reason I do not advise getting involved in formal incentive programs.

Oftentimes, referral incentive programs are materialistic and not personal, and frankly, you get the wrong type of referrals when they are paying to play. You want referrals for the right reasons. You want referral partners who are excited just because it feels good to be able to help those who they refer and help you too.

When it comes to incentives and motivation, you stand out because of your detective work uncovering your client preferences and documenting the details. If you decide to, you can tap into the personal motivations you uncovered in your detective work involving your partners' hobbies or your partners' special charities.

Be creative and look for ethical ways to direct funds. Wouldn't it be nice if you could help them achieve their charitable goals? Or it could be something very tangible, they are collectors of some sort.

I have a client who collects lighthouses. Whenever I see an artifact using a lighthouse theme, I have an opportunity to pick a personalized gift if I choose. The point is to make it personal.

Everyone's motivation is different. We talked about the Platinum Rule and how it is much better than the Golden Rule. The Golden Rule is good; in fact, it is a bible story reference. The Platinum Rule is just a little bit better. That "little bit" means a lot.

When you know what your client's motivations are, you avoid making assumptions. This is how you separate yourself from everyone else.

Always be on the lookout for hot buttons. In casual conversations, take notice when clients share their passions with you.

Document your observations in your customer relationship software. Review your files whenever you speak with your ideal clients and your referral partners. Continue to build your positioning and separate yourself from ordinary vendors and the ordinary sales professional. Knowing and using the Platinum Rule gives you an unfair advantage. You are developing your own algorithm as if you were a human computer. Do not depend on your memory.

There is work involved in keeping good records and you will be rewarded with the results you achieve because of the high-level service you provide. Not only will you increase your revenue, profits, or commissions, but you also increase your enjoyment of what you do for a living and how you do it. Loving your work should be at an all-time high; for many, that's much more valuable than financial reward.

PART 04

You now have three referral partners who love your work and are eager to continue to collaborate with you. You are a member of their business family.

We have established that you need to maintain good records to support your decisions.

We understand that teaching your idea clients how they can help you and further a mutually beneficial business relationship is the outcome you want to continue.

You have adopted the Platinum Rule and know how to zero in on each of your client's unique motivations to better serve them in the process. Your network is put together and you are now in the process of maintaining the effectiveness of your referral network.

When it comes to the relationship capital management, I want to expand our discussion of the concept of servant leadership. We have already discussed the idea that you are going to be serving your ideal clients at a high level, and you are going to be attending to their needs.

You are going to be documenting their unique motivation because you understand the Platinum Rule and look forward to collaborating with your clients and referral partners just the way they want.

An additional benefit of being a servant leader and being exclusive is you will begin to benefit from strong word of mouth advertising. Word of mouth advertising is the best form of advertising you could ever receive.

Without any additional effort, you are going to attract other similar types of people to you. It is up to you to determine whether you are going to include them in your partnership efforts. But for now, II would like to discuss how to maintain your momentum.

Sales professionals and companies in general frequently fall short of expectations in customer service. Your servant leadership will continue setting you apart. Continue to be creative by serving your clients in ways others cannot or will not.

Throughout the year, you will have multiple opportunities to touch people's lives and establish that you are a tremendous resource. Include in your record's what others neglect, like family details. For example, the size of their family, the names of their spouses, the names of their children and the entire family's birthdays. Now, you can reach out to family members on each occasion. It is just part of being attentive and friendly at a higher level. You are establishing a close connection.

As a servant leader, you see your clients as people in your care, first; clients, second. Keep communications business-like, but make it clear you pay attention to them as human beings. You just want to personalize your relationship as much as possible and appropriately.

It is not unusual to receive Christmas cards and birthday cards from vendors and other business relationships.

You set yourself apart by being aware of other life events by sending cards of congratulations, condolences, etc. One SYNER sends out Thanksgiving cards just because no one else does it.

No one else will typically pay attention to these details. In doing so, you give yourself another point of contact; by keeping you at the top of their mind.

In addition to sending out cards, there will be opportunities to acknowledge and share information regarding hobbies and charities as mentioned earlier. Everyone has passions, when you know what those are, you may find ways to feed into them with gestures and, gifts and donations if suitable.

Servant leadership is foreign today for some reason. The word servant is a negative word in a lot of people's minds, mostly because of ego. Especially in the selling profession, many are driven by ego. Setting your ego aside and focusing on the needs of others is powerful and raises your status in the minds of the people you serve. It is remarkably interesting that ego, usually is, an attempt to raise status. And servant leadership raises your status without you having to be egotistical. When you focus on serving, the results are always good. How could you not gain from doing the right thing? It is simply good business.

CHAPTER
09

SALES IN PRINT

PART 01

Salesmanship comes in many forms. And selling in print is an opportunity for sales professionals who are motivated to leverage all modes of communication. Copywriting is sales in print.

The first evidence of copywriting dates to Babylonian times in about 1477 where persuasive language was used to promote the sale of a prayer book. It is described as the act of writing a text for marketing or advertising purposes. The product of copywriting is referred to as copy. This piece of written content is designed to persuade people to act or to promote brand awareness.

Copywriters maintain some of the best writing and persuasion skills. They also have great research skills and an eye for headlines that benefit businesses of many kinds. The actual word "copywriting" means the act of writing words to sell products. The copywriter, often found in ad agencies or at home as a freelancer, is the person who does this.

Copywriting is fascinating; it is sales in print.

There are different claims for precisely how many types of copywriting exist. Besides general marketing copywriting, others include:

Email copywriting

Direct response copywriting (writing copy that has the goal of getting the reader to take an immediate action: purchase, sign up for a newsletter, follow on social media, etc.)

Social media copywriting

SEO copywriting

Technical copywriting

Copywriters craft words that sell and put together the right combination of benefit statements and words that trigger certain emotions for their intended readers / ideal clients. Then they create a close to get people to open their wallets.

Oftentimes, a successful sales letter or ad campaign could mean millions of dollars in sales to a company. Peter Drucker said, "The aim of marketing is to make selling superfluous." One sales letter written in such a way that resonates with its intended audience can do all the heavy lifting. Getting the intended readers' attention and interest creates desire and act with a letter! Crafting the right message, which resonates with its intended audience is exceedingly difficult. It takes about 10 years to become an A level copywriter. At this level, a copywriter can write his own ticket.

As a sales professional practicing servant leadership, you have an advantage. Because you are working with such a small group of people compared to what a copywriter normally would, you have tremendous insight into your client's personality and can use this information strategically. A copy writer typically does a great deal of product research, and then market research, before crafting a sales message. You have a head start!

When a copywriter has a winning sales idea, it is a home run for their clients. Copywriters write advertisements in print media, on the web, television, or radio. Imagine earning a small percentage of a marketing promotion when the sales volumes add up to multiple millions in sales.

Launched in 1988, Nike's "Just Do it" slogan was created and is credited with helping the brand increase its share of the North American market from $899 million to $9.2 billion over the following ten years. That is just one sales message, one slogan. How did such a simple yet brief message do so well? It is not easy to say, but you can imagine. Because the target audience was athletes of all types, the brevity, and the emphasis on taking action was the right trigger!

Copywriters research market segments and use storytelling, emotional persuasion, brevity, and uniqueness to create millions of dollars of revenue when they are successful.

When crafting a story, the most important thing is to understand who your audience is. What are their hot points? What are they trying to achieve? How can you (and your brand) help them achieve their goals? You can bet that the images in all the Nike ads emphasized an athlete going a bit farther in their shoe!

You too can leverage the power of storytelling in all modes of your communications. People enjoy hearing stories around real-life experiences; your testimonials and personal success stories can be repurposed in other formats like email marketing, for example.

As sales professionals, we intuitively select our words carefully. We all have our favorite words and phrases and use them with our clients.

While we are looking at an exceedingly small audience in comparison, we can be even more successful percentagewise when we know our markets and our clients intimately. We can be even more precise in addressing our client's passions, emotions, and motivations.

Your favorite one-liners and your favorite closes should be documented, measured, and evaluated. Marketers and copywriters know that one approach can outperform another exponentially. Copywriters will send two different messages sometimes, using just a different headline and learn that one headline outperforms the other tenfold. Changing a simple headline can be the difference between a company's marketing being a total success, or a major bust.

I am not saying that as a sales professional you should be expert at copywriting or sales in print; what I am saying is that, as a SYNER, you need to recognize the power of your words at a higher level. If you have been selling for any length of time, you already have some language you know works.

I suggest that you write your best sales language down, test one approach against another. Over a month's time, measure the results. Consumer demands and interests are a moving target. We need to stay on top of the changes in the needs and desires of our markets and change accordingly.

I suggest you take a tape recorder and record your best sales presentation, have it transcribed, and use the key elements in your sales presentation in your emails and your voice mails to evaluate one approach against another.

If you are sending out letters and postcards, use the best language. Create these types of communications in greeting cards wherever it deems appropriate. There's tremendous power using the right words at the right time.

"The difference between the almost right word and the right word is really a large matter-Tis the difference between the lightning bug and lightning." ~ Mark Twain. The point is that your words should not be taken lightly. Therefore, repurpose your sales speak and use it intentionally and in different modes of communication.

If you are comfortable with writing, you can use copywriting in your local newspapers writing advertisements, write articles in industry trade magazines with a call to action, write direct response sales letters to generate leads and or sales, write radio ads and negotiate airtime on local radio and write advertising for digital ads on Google, FaceBook or LinkedIn.

The data you store in your CRM software will give you several keywords you can use in your communications with clients and improve your results. Remember, when we use the language of our client's, we improve our connection.

Every top producer has language that is their own and separates them from 80% of their competition. What you say and how you say it can sometimes be overlooked. One thing you have in your favor is that, when you see yourself as a servant leader and exercise the Platinum Rule, finding the right thing to say becomes easy.

Look at wordsmithing like this: The difference between a first-place horse and a second-place horse might be a nose, but the prize money can be thousands, if not tens of thousands of dollars depending on the stakes. The same holds true with saying the right word and the wrong word in your communications. These small details mean so much.

> ➢ Track your closing ratio when selling to referrals and consistently evaluate different sales approaches to continue to improve, because consumer markets are always changing.

> ➢ Take your knowledge of what works best and show referral partners the right thing to say and track the effectiveness of any scripts.

> ➢ Perfect the words you use to communicate because they are assets, and the more you recognize the power of your spoken word, the more effective you will be. As sales professionals, we often overlook the power of our words.

It will not hurt you to look at the copywriting profession and become more familiar with the craft.

If you dig deeper into copywriting history, you will find fledgling companies that turned the corner because of a single sales promotion, a storyline, slogan, mission statement, tagline, or a headline written with the right elements, and turned the company around.

It makes sense to point out the power of salesmanship in its many forms to get you thinking about areas of opportunity for yourself, as a SYNER.

PART 02

Now, you are better suited for optimizing and continually evaluating one of your methods against another. There is always a better way to do something. You want to find it before your competitor does.

Direct marketers and copywriters use testing constantly. Use at least a minimum of two different approaches and measure the results. Being relevant, and consistently improving allows you to maintain your value.

Use your customer relation management software and your detailed notes to help you leverage your communications as much as possible. At this point, you are aware and conscious of how effective the language you are using can be! One approach is always better than another. When the winner emerges, you concentrate on using the winner.

When you see a drop in your results, you can continue to evaluate. A winner does not stay at winner forever.

Markets are constantly changing, people are born, mature and die, technology changes, new competitors enter the market, etc.

We do not want to be trendy, but we do not want to miss a major shift in the thinking of our target audience either. If you look at consumer products in general, every year, there is a new product, or a new slogan promoting an established product. Marketers know they must stay current, and so should you.

Always look for a competitive edge, otherwise, you run the risk of losing touch with the attitudes and preferences of your clients.

Constantly stay in contact with your key referral partners and pay close attention to their experiences. Converse with your ideal clients, and other vendors who serve the same market that you serve. Always, be in market research mode. Your new SYNER mentality is to consistently look for constant and never-ending opportunities for improvement; this changes your thinking drastically. You do not want to lose touch with your audience; this is how you enjoy longevity in your career and stay on top of the action.

CHAPTER
10
NETWORKING
STRATEGICALLY

PART 01

Networking is something that I avoided early in my career because it looked like bootlicking to me, and my ego would not allow me to associate with people just because I wanted something from them. I prided myself for being a bootstrapper. I was competitive and felt I did not need help from influencers. "You get yours and I will get mine" was my mantra.

The concept of schmoozing people to make an impression put a bad taste in my mouth. My ego made me do things the hard way and I was proud of it because I had success pounding the pavement, making more dials, etc.

I was roughing it out and feeling a sense of pride because I was a tough guy. But my perspective was wrong and shortsighted; you might even say I was missing out tremendously because I did not know how business really worked. I did not understand leverage.

But now I understand that networking is not collecting contacts and asking for things, it is nurturing relationships.

Archimedes was the philosopher who is credited for saying "Give Me a Lever Long Enough and I Can Move the World."

When you network with influencers, people who have a tremendous following and lots of credibility and who may be where you are striving to get to, you can only help yourself.

Here is what I learned, there is a right way and a wrong way to network, and I did not know the difference. I eventually figured out where I was wrong. And hopefully, my awakening will save someone from having to go through the same learning process.

I would listen to me if I were you because I figured it out and I could save you a ton of time and a lot of anguish which brings us to why you want to identify people who have a tremendous influence.

Influencers make excellent clients and even better referral partners. A lot of these influencers have taken decades to build their credibility. And by associating yourself with these sorts of people, you could shave years of struggle out of your career.

Your business will grow much faster, so you want to identify who the folks are in your community or in your immediate network. Find the centers of influence, size them up, and figure out if they have a large enough audience where it is worth building a relationship.

Make sure influencers are ethical and have a bond with their tribes, because what you are after is to leverage relationships that make sense for you.

PART 02

We talked about why you want to identify influencers and how powerful they can be. We did not get into how you make that work. The good news is you do not have to be a groupie. You do not have to look like a beggar, a pan handler, or a green pea.

The key is giving to get. Hold on to in your mind, the future version of yourself where you see yourself having great influence because this is where you are going with this process. You are already building value in the service you provide to your ideal clients, add the influencers who meet your criteria to your database.

Whether you connect with influencers or not, it pays to know what they are communicating to their tribe. Pay attention to their motivations. Pay attention to what they are trying to accomplish and when you see the opportunity, support their efforts.

When it is convenient, support the influencer by attending their events. Supporting their causes and sharing information with your clients and with the influencer if you suspect the information might be valuable to them.

When you share information, let them know you thought she might be interested in this data because you have been following them for some time and know their passions. In time, you will be viewed as an ally, colleague, or peer. Be supportive and use your customer relationship software package to make sure that you are nurturing that relationship frequently. You are positioning yourself as someone who is a resource; not a beggar, not a pan handler, not a green pea, but someone who is a resource that can be depended on for accurate and relevant information. This is a long-term strategy but can be shortened when you demonstrate great value.

When you are presenting yourself as someone who is committed to the industry and focused on professionalism, at some point, they are going to acknowledge you for it and reciprocate; you may not even have to ask.

It may sound a little off to say that you are giving to get; what you are really doing is you are taking advantage of the law of reciprocity. You cannot help someone without helping yourself. Even if you do not get a formal acknowledgement or endorsement, just maintaining an association with people who have a high-level credibility rubs off on you.

The Law of Reciprocity is part of the psychology of influence and simply states that there is a desire to give back in kind when receiving an unexpected gift.

You are a part of the mix; you are in the middle of all the action. Do everything you can to maintain a presence and you will earn your brass, one way or the other.

Before long, it will be appropriate for you to ask for a letter of introduction to the influencers' constituents because you have established yourself as someone who has value, who is a giver, and who is exercising the Platinum Rule.

You understand servant leadership; and that how as a follower, you cannot be a leader and ask people to follow you, unless you know how to follow.

You may even choose to associate with multiple influencers but beware, you do not want to be overwhelmed. Being supportive of others does take some time.

SERVANT LEADERS

- See leadership as an opportunity to serve others.
- Share power and control to drive engagement.
- Measures success through relationship growth and development
- Listen to what is said and unspoken.
- Understand it is not about them.

So depending on your time management skill, you may want to pick one or two influencers.

Good leaders were once good followers. You want to follow the influencers of your choice. In time, you will begin to see patterns and see yourself as an equal, as you notice how they have succeeded.

You will notice their preferences, who influenced them, their quirks, and motivations, and document what you learn in your relationship management software.

At the appropriate time, you make them aware that you know what their sensitivities are. You earn their respect by identifying that you are not just someone that flies by night. Instead, you are attentive to the people in your circle. It will be quite easy to endorse you and your products once they witness your value.

You are an excellent follower; and at some point, you become a leader in the eyes of your niche-you become one of the influencers. So if you have not figured it out yet, this book is for someone who is playing the long game, plans to have longevity and long-term success. Short-term strategies have their place, but they are really designed for people who are not thinking beyond their next paycheck. Long game strategy requires vision and is simple if you are organized.

PART 03

So now you know the importance of networking with influencers. There is great leverage when you gain access to their network, which may have taken them decades to build. Networking is particularly valuable if you plan to stay in your industry long term.

If you ever change jobs, you take your influencer relationships with you. Their power is transferable, so once again, staying in your industry gives you a lot of leverage. Relationships you create with your ideal clients may also follow you, depending on the strength of the relationship.

One of the ways to choose influencers is to look at your SWOT analysis. Look at your strong points and your personality to find influencers you resonate with. The chances of you clicking increase, and your ability to leverage their influence increases dramatically if you are somebody they like.

Being a person of color, I will point out that race is less important than personality. Personality is everything. When you bring value to the table, you circumvent all preconceived notions.

Value is a language understood by everyone. Always bring value with your professionalism—insight is transferable across cultures. This attitude will carry you throughout your career.

Your honesty in completing your SWOT will help you determine where you need to grow. You want to look at themes. If you were not thorough in completing your SWOT analysis, go back and fine tune your assessment of yourself. In your SWOT analysis, you may find common interests you share with people you identify as influencers.

Leverage your personality; for example, if you are an analytical person who thinks in numbers, it makes sense for you to look for influencers who also speak in numbers.

If you are a conceptual thinker or have an expressive personality, you will not be compatible with someone who is analytical, unless you identify the differences you share and change how you interact with this person. Remember the Platinum Rule and treat people how they would like to be treated. In this case, focus on speaking their language.

There are entire courses and books on personality differences and how to improve relationships with people with different personalities. I have given you enough to put personality theory into play. However, if you want to dig deeper, take one of the tests online or find a book on the topic.

The point is you want to find people you resonate with. When two like minds are brought together, a third mind is created—ideas just seem to flow. Ideally, you find influencers you genuinely admire and support. Your admiration will come through when you communicate with them, and they can tell you are a kindred spirit.

The influencers you identify may be local, if so, you can get face to face with them by taking them out to lunch or dinner. But more likely, you are going to use social media to connect. The social media websites most appropriate for business are going to be Twitter, LinkedIn, and YouTube.

The subject of social media marketing is worthy of a book of its own. However, it is important to know that influencers have preferences for how they communicate. You are one step ahead when you know their preferred modes of communication.

Social media modes of communication preferred by serious business- people are LinkedIn and Twitter. YouTube is ideal for those influencers who are visual and realize that video is the most powerful mode of communication on the web. You may benefit from using video and by communicating with visually oriented influencers.

I am not saying that you should be a YouTuber, but you certainly want to be a subscriber to their YouTube channel, making comments on their posts, sending messages, sharing content and insights. But mostly, bring them value and build a relationship.

CHAPTER
11
PUTTING EVEN MORE
PEOPLE TOGETHER

PART 01

So far, you have been introduced to the importance of relationship capital development as it applies to referral marketing, and how a few of your ideal clients may make great referral partners because of their influence.

We have also explored what influencers in your industry, your community, and anyone that you have contact with who has more access to your ideal clients than you, can do to get you more exposure.

We gave you a winning strategy to get their respect and gain access to their tribes.

You now know how to approach influencers from a position of strength and avoid groveling for their support. If all I did was help you develop referral partners out of your ideal clients and one or two relationships with influencers in your marketplace, that could be enough to make you a solid player in your profession.

You have learned two avenues, ideal client referral partners, and influencers in your niche you can use to bring quality leads on a regular basis. If you end up with the fortunate problem of being overwhelmed by leads because of your success, you could divert some of your leads to other salespeople for a fee or a percentage.

If this is the case, you will have other salespeople in your industry working on your behalf, taking the clients that you cannot service because you are too busy. Being overwhelmed by leads is a problem that most people would love to have.

Caution! Make sure you are within your company policies before selling away to other salespeople. If your mindset is that something is better than nothing, then sharing commissions and profits with other salespeople makes sense.

The typical salesperson who does not use marketing and self-promotion strategies typically has only one method for creating leads; and most of the time, that one strategy is not efficient. You are in a better place. You have learned two high quality, very strategic and high yielding activities to bring leads into your business. At a minimum, you must **master** Referral Marketing using Ideal Clients, this should be your priority.

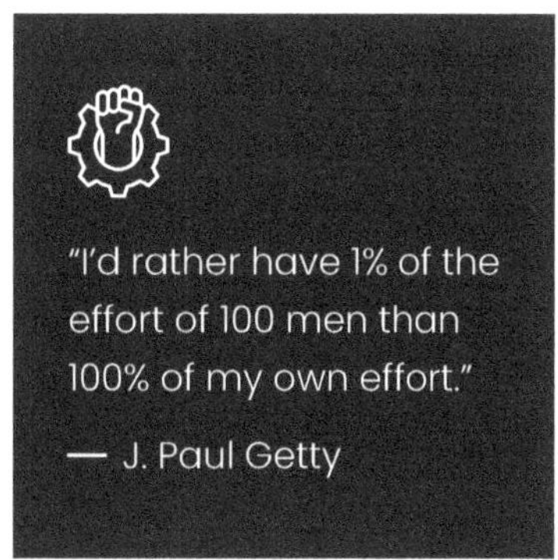

You can continue to nurture your ideal client referral partner relationships and gradually increase their yield, or you can add more arrows to your quiver and develop even more marketing avenues to create clients. If you want even more growth opportunities, read on. Let us look at other potential avenues for bringing high quality clients to you.

The first tactic I want to introduce to you is joint venturing. Think of a product that is naturally purchased before or after someone purchases your product. Let us just think in terms of accessories; something that you do not offer but another vendor does, and it is a product your ideal client would buy before or after purchasing your offer are potential joint venture partners.

So how do you go about creating a joint venture relationship? You just ask. But before you ask, educate your potential partners that you are not competing against each other. In fact, together, we could create a mutually advantageous relationship simply by sharing our clients.

For example, this is going to be oversimplified but it helps paint the picture. So if I sell paint, but I do not sell brushes, it makes sense for me to have a relationship with the best distributor of brushes and it makes sense for him to have a relationship with me.

My customers need brushes, his customers need paint, so we figure out a way to work together. I spend a day in his office with products, or I just have product in his showroom and vice versa, or maybe we do joint activities together, or we do trade shows together. Most vendors in this industry already sell both, but you get the idea.

Think outside the box and figure out what ancillary or which accessory products will compliment what you are selling. If I am a computer salesman, we all know that computers require software. Typically, when you visit a computer store, they have some software, but they do not sell it; it is just sitting there.

Upselling and cross selling are part of servant leadership in sales because you do not want to underserve your clients. Always show them their options.

Joint ventures are different. You will be adding product purchases that are not typically upselling or cross selling opportunities.

Let us say you sell residential real estate and have preferred service providers who clean houses, clean carpets, landscape, clean pools, and mobile car detailers. You could connect these service providers and they may have opportunities to get listings for you as well. You may or may not negotiate a percentage of the sale. You will negotiate a discounted rate for your customers and continue to build goodwill.

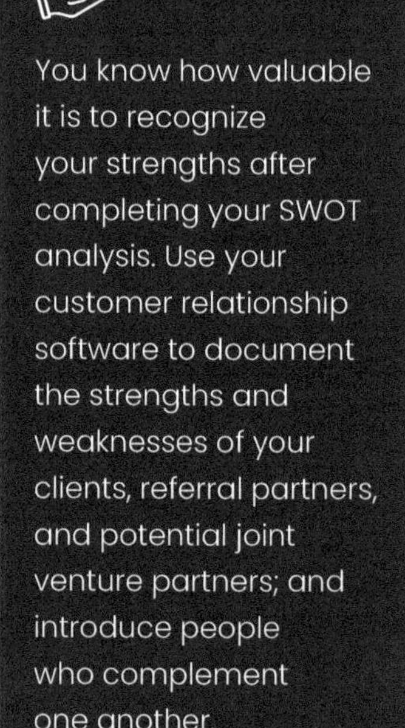

Think of products and services that are usually not packaged with your sale but should be and put people together. The sales effort is typically very minimal, but everyone profits when properly negotiated in advance.

A lot of good car salesman have a relationship with a property and casualty insurance agent; this is because they make an agreement in advance. The car salesman will introduce his customers to his preferred auto insurance provider, and they compensate each other and vice versa.

Brainstorm the possibilities. If you come up short on ideas, one way to find out is to ask your clients what their other needs are. If you cannot serve those needs, find someone else who can and become the connection between two brands.

PART 02

We are on a roll! We talked about building your network of referral partners created from the top 20% of your clients, these are your ideal clients. We know that if we are serious players, we can influence the influencers in our industry if we choose. You have learned that servitude is leadership in training. You nurture relationships by being a supporter, follower and then an influencer yourself.

You know your value and are confident in arranging joint ventures with compatible sellers who are non- competing.

There is no limit to what you can create for yourself when you have the mindset. You recognize that when you reach out to people, all your communications have varying degrees of value. As a synergistic sales and marketing professional, you know that the words you choose create a result. The result can be good, better, and then best when you evaluate. So, choose your words strategically.

Keep your eyes open and be mindful of all the opportunities that surround you everywhere. Hopefully, this book will open your eyes to so many possibilities and you will be able to pick out the ones that mean the most to you and fit your personality and your skillset.

Additionally, I have two more ideas I want to share with you. The first of which is, how do you create positive word of mouth?

You have seen the power of word of mouth in your everyday lives. When an idea goes viral on the internet, it takes on a life of its own. You could spend tens of thousands of dollars and never get as much attention as a successful word of mouth experience.

The likelihood of you benefiting from of viral communication, a viral meme, or an advertisement going viral is minuscule. However, if you do not play the game, you are guaranteed not to win or do anything that can go viral.

So how do you give yourself a chance? You encourage your satisfied clients to share their experiences with you on social media.

Whichever social media platform they participate in, have them share success stories, or funny events that take place during day-to-day activities. Be mindful that people are attracted to humor—people want to be entertained.

So when something entertaining happens in your business, do not waste it. Encourage sharing stories on social media and who knows, you might be one of the very few who benefit from something that goes viral!

The second opportunity comes in the form of public relations. We have already talked about influencers, but there are opportunities to take advantage of mass media, and even through leaders on the internet.

Be aware of radio and TV programs your ideal clients consume also, podcasters and bloggers relevant to your business.

Pay attention to their topics of discussion, their thinking, their storylines, what types of stories are important to them. You may even find buzz in local newspapers and trade magazines. Pay attention to writers who are specialists on your topic. If you can feed them a story, do so!

When you feel you know their interests, think in terms of the Platinum Rule, you can reach out to these personalities and ask them if it will help them if you share your insight with them?

You always want to come from the position of wanting to help and be supportive. Think Servitude. A simple call or letter could suffice. If you want to be formal, you could hire someone to write a press release, whatever works. Keep in mind that these personalities must keep fresh ideas and often need new story ideas, so you will be helpful when you position yourself correctly.

If you can write, submitting articles and stories involving your business could be interesting. Once again, you are going to have to look at your skill set—see your SWOT.

If you are a writer, you may want to ask for an opportunity to guest host or guest write a blog post or be interviewed. You have the gift of gab and can speak in public; you may have value suitable for an appearance on radio show or a podcast.

Approach these people the same way you approach influencers. Provide them with insight and share information with them. Let them know that you might have something they are interested in learning. Express that you do not know for sure, but you thought you would ask because you are a regular listener, or a regular reader or subscriber and you thought they might be interested in something that you are doing and so you decided to approach them in the appropriate way.

Sometimes, it is just as simple as picking up the phone and calling in to see if you can get the producer on the phone. Nothing ventured, nothing gained. You want to monitor whatever these professionals are doing because there is potential for you to leverage the relationship they have with their audience. If they decide that you have something that is newsworthy and they promote what you are doing, you are in a tremendous position to gain great exposure.

Retain copies of all your successes collaborating with these folks and build a portfolio because once you have done a podcast or a radio show, or you have been mentioned in an article or in a trade magazine, your value rises. Everybody likes a winner—somebody who has previously gained exposure makes it easier to gain more.

If you do well with the media, who knows where your success will take you. More professional content creators may want to get in on the action and invite you to contribute to their audiences.

Once you get the snowball rolling, it becomes larger and larger as it rolls down the hill; this is simply a metaphor for what can happen if you strike the right nerve with one of these media personalities.

For the right SYNER, media exposure may be a potential avenue you can take to get leads for your business and a whole lot more. The marketing activities I present to you will stimulate your thinking and help you to see yourself as an intrapreneur. You may even evolve from being an employee into a business owner.

PART 03

Media Kit

I want to share with you a quote from Nelson Mandela; he said, "There is no passion to be found playing small in settling for a life that is less than the one you are capable of living." I say, if you are going to play, you might as well play to win. Shoot for the stars and if you miss, at least you hit the moon.

So, in saying that, prepare for opportunities that might come your way especially if you start contacting people in the media.

Keep up your awareness and when the opportunity comes, leverage public relations opportunities. PR is free, but it is not easy to get. But when you see an angle, you want to be prepared.

You should have at a minimum, a media kit which is not that complicated; it is just documents that you can share electronically or by mail to anyone who wants to know your story.

There are three pieces that are required. You can add more, but these three are the most important: Firstly, you should have someone write your short biography, remember when we discussed your SWOT analysis, and sales and print. Emphasize your unique personality and your personal brand.

I know for some people it can be difficult to engage in self-promotion. A tip for finding your value is to ask your peers, clients, and managers what it is that they appreciate about you. Use the feedback as a foundation and put your most valuable and unique attributes in writing.

Collect the information you could not have said about yourself and have someone else write it. The biography does not have to be long; it could be a paragraph, a page or a page and a half.

You want the words to have impact, differentiating yourself, making you stand out, and highlighting your unique personality.

Every one of us is different; you want to highlight your uniqueness. Just like there are no two snowflakes alike, and no two fingerprints, there are no two people alike.

When it comes to self-promotion, you need to zero in on how you are different and how you are unique— that is how you eliminate competition. You are always selling yourself. There is no other you, align your uniqueness with the value you provide.

Secondly, you want to have a photograph that can be reproduced in case a print publication or even a website wants to show your picture.

My suggestion is that you take several photos, a standard portrait, something hokey, and something that you know makes people laugh.

Depending on what you sell, you may want a photo with a prop or a photo with your products. Choose something that makes you look different, something that makes you look interesting. These photos do not have to be expensive, the quality of cell phones these days is all you need.

You could download an app from Walmart or Walgreens and have your photos printed through the app and pick them up at your leisure.

You could hire a professional and have your photo shot with a professional background, it is your choice. Just make sure that it is a photo that you appreciate and that others will too.

The photos can be black and white or color or both. I do not think photography is that expensive these days, why not have both?

Last, but not least, you should be collecting testimonials. The more testimonials, the better. Make sure they represent exactly what you are trying to communicate. Video testimonials are best for online and printed testimonials are good in every mode, so it is best to have both.

If you do collect video testimonies, you want to get a release because you are using someone's image, and you want to make sure that you are not infringing on someone's copyright. All you need is a signed statement that says you have permission to use the video and images you are sharing, and that is about all that is required. (Consult with an attorney if you have more involved issues with copyright)

If you like, you could take it a step further and have letters of reference included in your kit. They cannot hurt—they would be the 4th item.

If you have in your skill set the ability to do public speaking, having film clips of you speaking to a group of customers, or speaking at a Rotary meeting, or at a sales meeting will go a long way in illustrating how you might look on camera and sound to listeners.

If you have the opportunity, use video. Have the video professionally edited. It does not have to have music but if you add music, it could make it more dramatic and more impactful.

Media kits can be email or snail mailed depending on the situation. Now if you have successfully nurtured a relationship with an influencer or member of the media, you can give them what they need to get you coverage. You can also distribute these to bloggers, in addition to local radio personalities and television media.

If you can produce a newsworthy angle, you may get the opportunity to be involved in a local morning television broadcast or even the evening news. Nothing ventured, nothing gained. It pays to think big. The media kit is going to help get you in the door.

12

LETTER TO MY READER

PART 01

You have taken a masterful journey into what I call synergistic salesmanship, mixing the disciplines of selling and marketing together. If you are a consultative or a needs-based sales professional, adding marketing to your toolbox allows you to exponentially build your business in the cleverest and most strategic and professional way by learning to profit from your good will.

You have identified how to create your own personal brand. If you have not realized it already, you are now equipped to perform at a high level without having to ever compromise integrity.

Some people in sales find themselves conflicted at times and sacrifice their integrity to make a sale. I do not see a conflict; it is the only way to go.

You have also identified where most salespeople are missing the boat, they are just not good at creating their own leads. My brand of referral marketing gives you tremendous leverage.

This is the reason a marketing education makes sense. When you look at what you do as a marketer, by crafting your sales persona, by looking deep into who you are and who you want to serve, you will see where you will adjust and improve your effectiveness.

You may find you are not properly aligned with the right product or the right company. This alignment is what you need to make everything come together.

Continue to look at your SWOT analysis. You certainly want to focus on your strong points to point you in the right direction and help you tap into your personal power.

If your weaknesses need to be shored up, or you need to close your knowledge gap, you now have the motivation to do so because you want to provide high level services and products.

To be confident in the activities you have learned in this book, you must be competent. Optimism alone will not carry you. As a realist, you must know your limitations, you must know what works and what does not work.

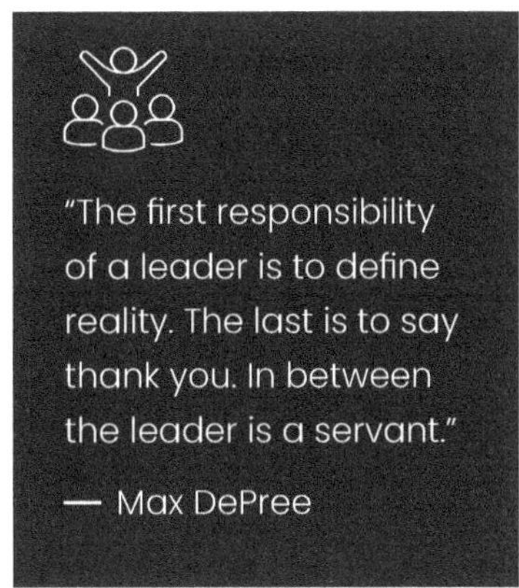

You have also learned that you should be investing most of your time with clients who fit your personal criteria. Continue to refine how you define your ideal client. Once you are clear about who is the best fit for you, you will be positioned to advance a step further and figure out which of these clients would be ideal referral partners. What I teach is not typically found in a company provided sales training program, what you have just learned will certainly give you a chance to take your sales activities to a new level.

The Platinum Rule is powerful. You can rely on succeeding by doing what is best for your clients.

Turn the rule on yourself and gain even more power during goal setting. Being properly aligned with what is most important to you and the people that are important in your life gives your goals tremendous momentum.

We took a deep look at 80/20. The Pareto Principle and how everything is affected by 80/20. At the very beginning of the book, I pointed out that over 80% of clients or consumers who have made purchases are willing to give referrals, and only about 29% of salespeople even ask.

When I talk to salespeople, they often tell me they get their share of referrals, but what they are really saying is they are taking advantage of all the accidental referrals they receive. This is not initiative-taking, and there is no attention given to the quality of the referral.

The majority or 80% of salespeople really do not know how to cultivate a referral marketing program; and that is the major gift I have given you.

We have taken your business a step further by teaching you how to optimize your activities. By making sure you know your sales numbers, evaluating one approach against another for continual growth. You can now scale your numbers by borrowing tactics from the marketing world.

You know the markets are constantly changing, and by evaluating your approaches against each other, it allows you to zero in on the activities that give you the highest yields and the most profitable. You are continually working to improve those numbers.

We looked at the copywriting profession and how copywriters use sales language in print.

Copywriters can have massive results, finding consumer hot buttons, focusing on using the right words at the right time, and making millions for advertisers. You are armed with this information, and you now know how to take your words more seriously than in the past.

Pay more attention to details and use customer relationship management software to document your observations.

You are better positioned now because you document your client's motivations, habits, and hobbies to continually allow you to serve your clients at a higher level.

We looked at networking and how for me and many others, networking resembled bootlicking until I figured out how to network strategically from the position of servitude.

We now know that servant leadership is not only for serving your clients; it is for serving the colleagues you want to be aligned with as equals. There are two types of people: givers and takers. You want influencers in your network to see you as a person of value, someone who is always offering a helping hand.

Always look for opportunities to make small value deposits into your client relationships, and into influencers businesses and support their objectives.

Establish yourself as an asset making deposits into others' lives well before taking out any withdrawals. In fact, you do not deserve to ask for anything from influencers unless you have first earned their respect.

Servant leadership gives you the opportunity to earn respect—the respect of your peers and colleagues in your industry. This approach holds true when working with media personalities as well.

When you look at yourself, evaluate how you are perceived by your clients versus your self-perception. Presenting yourself one way might be better than another.

PART 02

I am super excited for you for taking this journey. When the stars are in alignment, meaning when you know your strong points, you know your limitations. You are positioned to succeed—armed with the best version of yourself, preparing to win on a playing field where you have advantages.

You know what you need to do to move ahead. Once you have everything congruent with who you are as a person, when you are being authentic, it will appear that you have the Midas Touch.

You will be a leader of a smooth operation—an operation that utilizes leverage at every opportunity.

You are no longer a single entity; you have leverage enlisting support from referral partners. You have influencers in your network that you are continually building. No one builds anything meaningful alone. It always takes a community and a team.

You now know how to build your team, manage relationships in such a way that prepares them to support you when the time is right.

The Platinum Rule is your secret weapon. You are going to find a lot of ways to apply the Platinum Rule.

Once you get in the habit of serving people using "The Rule," you will be surprised how you set yourself apart. Too many people are self-centered. Your constituents will be impressed by how much you know about their likes and dislikes and how you cater to their needs.

You are on your way to becoming a sales leader on your terms. Imagine how your willingness to be a servant of people who are the best fit for you could **bring you** so much value. Servitude leads to leadership, and your ability to grow your expertise and influence will solidify you as the go to guy amongst the people in your niche.

One of the most interesting attributes of being in sales is you often hear that selling is one of the highest paying professions—a profession limited only by the size of your imagination. You now have the tools to expand your imagination and your earnings.

You can now bring value like you have never done before. You are in a position of strength. You will not need to focus on doing much asking for help; people naturally would want to reciprocate. It is the law of reciprocity, which is the way it is. Typically, when you give, people just want to give in return.

Every action we take will be met with some type of reaction by another person. There is a deep-rooted psychological urge to do something in return when people are treated well. The energy you send often returns in even greater magnitude.

When you are constantly sharing information and bringing value to people's lives, specifically those that you deliberately want to focus on, you are not going to have to do a lot of asking.

Your activities as a servant leader will prompt people to ask how they might be able to help you? And when that happens, you know you are in the driver's seat. If you have made it this far, then you will appreciate what I am about to tell you.

I expect this book will be a great revelation for many. I know that 80% of the market does not think the way that I am thinking. There is not anything new in this book; what is new are the combinations of concepts brought together to form a new mentality.

The information I have put together will create new ways of looking at your sales career, so this is what you should do next.

Do not make the mistake of just reading this book and putting it down and relying on the less than 20% that you are going to remember in the days ahead.

There are studies that suggest that you will remember about 10% of what you have read after about one week, so dig deep into the concepts in this book and study what you have learned. Studying is underrated. If it is true that repetition is the mother of learning, you serve yourself better by reviewing the ideas in this book regularly.

Do not cut corners in doing the SWOT analysis. If you need to, ask people who know you best to criticize you as tough as they can.

Then collect compliments; you want to make sure you get it straight. A lot of times, people will tell you only what they think you want to hear, dig deep into self-analysis.

Knowledge of self is the foundation for growth. Once you have your self-analysis, you can decide whether you are positioned properly for your skillset or not.

You will have to modify your situation, switch products, geographies, companies, etc. I do not know what those are for you, but these are things that you are going to evaluate as you work through the SWOT analysis. Once you are clear about your own attributes, you can build on them.

The next thing you want to do is identify who your ideal clients are. Provide as much detail as possible. For example, consider their occupation, gender, age, marital status, income, and geography. Find as many criteria as possible—do not leave it up to guess work.

If you are not sure, experiment by working with two distinctly different categories of people over a month or a fiscal quarter. Pay attention to which group of people responds to you and your marketing message the best.

The next step, assuming you have made sales to multiple groups of people, is to figure out which 20% of your clients fit your ideal client profile.

Do your best to segment your clients. Put them into different categories so you can do strategic discrimination. And yes, you should be discriminate against who you invest your time in and provide services for.

Discriminate further by making sure that you know which of your ideal clients with influence are in the top 20% of your top 20%. This 4% of your clients represent your superstars.

Your Superstars will be where you are going to invest your time. These superstars are where you will create referral cultures and your future growth. You will monitor their success and help them succeed in helping their people, and in turn, you will help yourself. Thank you for investing your time to learn what synergistic sales and marketing looks like. For additional resources please see the appendix.

About the Author

Valdez Lasartemay began selling at a young age going door to door selling newspaper subscriptions for the San Francisco Chronicle. Throughout his career he has sold everything from shoes to securities and everything in between. Selling was a career choice made while in college when he discovered that selling allows you to get paid what you are worth and avoid glass ceilings, nepotism, racism, and all the other isms. When it comes to sales all that people care about is how you perform. While the playing field is not always fair, with the proper motivation and strategy, he feels that everyone can be successful by fine tuning their ability to communicate what is good. Adding tactics and strategies borrowed from the fields of marketing and negotiation is advancing professionalism in selling. Today, Valdez's motivation is to be the man he wished he knew when he first began to sell. While selling has evolved over the years one thing that always sells is excellence.

Appendix

Servant Leadership

THE ULTIMATE MARKETING TOOL

In business, leadership is not just about guiding a team to meet its goals; it is about inspiring individuals to reach their full potential while fostering a culture of trust, collaboration, and innovation. One leadership philosophy that has gained significant traction in recent years is servant leadership. This approach, which emphasizes serving others before oneself, is not just a noble philosophy but also a powerful marketing tool. In this article, we will define servant leadership, present a case for its role as the ultimate marketing tool, and outline best practices for embracing this leadership style.

DEFINING SERVANT LEADERSHIP:

Servant leadership is a leadership philosophy that focuses on the well-being and development of team members primarily. It was coined by Robert K. Greenleaf in his essay "The Servant as Leader" in 1970 and has since gained recognition as a transformational approach to leadership.

AT ITS CORE, SERVANT LEADERSHIP IS ABOUT:

Putting People First: Servant leaders prioritize the needs and growth of their team members, empowering them to achieve their highest potential.

Empathy and Compassion: They show deep empathy and compassion toward their team, understanding their individual strengths, weaknesses, and aspirations.

Servitude: Servant leaders actively serve their team, removing obstacles, providing guidance, and fostering a positive work environment.

THE CASE FOR SERVANT LEADERSHIP AS THE ULTIMATE MARKETING TOOL:

Now, you may wonder how a leadership philosophy can serve as a marketing tool. The connection lies in the fact that authentic servant leadership can have a profound impact on an organization's brand, reputation, and customer loyalty. Here is why it is the ultimate marketing tool:

Trust and Credibility: When leaders genuinely care about their employees' well-being and success, it fosters a culture of trust within the organization. This trust extends to customers, who are more likely to engage with and purchase from a company that values its people.

Employee Advocacy: Servant leaders inspire their team members to become enthusiastic brand advocates. Happy employees who believe in their company's values are more likely to share their positive experiences with friends, family, and on social media, thereby enhancing the brand's reputation.

Innovation and Problem-Solving: Servant leadership encourages a culture of collaboration and open communication. This environment can lead to greater innovation and the ability to respond effectively to customer needs and challenges.

Customer-Centric Focus: Servant leaders prioritize customer needs and satisfaction by first ensuring that their employees are content and motivated. This commitment to customer-centricity naturally aligns with marketing efforts.

BEST PRACTICES FOR SERVANT LEADERSHIP:

Embracing servant leadership as a marketing tool requires a concerted effort and the following best practices:

Lead by Example: Demonstrate the behaviors and values you want to see in your team. Show empathy, humility, and a willingness to serve.

Listen Actively: Practice active listening to understand your team's concerns, ideas, and aspirations. Make it clear that their voices are heard and valued.

Empower and Develop: Provide opportunities for growth and development and encourage autonomy and responsibility among team members.

Remove Obstacles: Identify and eliminate obstacles that hinder your team's productivity and success.

Communicate Transparently: Maintain open and honest communication with your team. Share the organization's vision, goals, and challenges.

Recognize and Appreciate: Acknowledge and appreciate the contributions of your team members regularly. Celebrate their successes and milestones.

Embrace Diversity and Inclusion: Foster an inclusive workplace that values diversity of thought and background.

Lead for the Long Term: Servant leadership is a long-term commitment. Continuously strive to improve and evolve your leadership style.

In conclusion, servant leadership goes beyond just managing a team; it transforms an organization's culture and impacts its relationship with customers. By genuinely serving and empowering your team, you create a compelling brand story that resonates with customers, making servant leadership the ultimate marketing tool in today's business landscape.

Relationship Capital Management Benefits

RETENTION

A U.S. News and World Report study found that the average American business loses 15% of its customer base each year.

A Bain and Company/Harvard Business Review study found that a 5% increase in customer retention can increase profits between 25% and 100% percent.

What is sad for you and me is that most of those customers who leave because of a customer service issue do not bother to complain. The study concludes:

➤ 68% of customers who stop buying from one business and go to another do so because of poor or indifferent service.

➤ 14% leave because of an unsatisfactorily resolved dispute or complaint.

REFERRALS

The Wharton School of Business reports 83% of customers want to give a referral. Only 29% do because customers are not being asked for referrals by salespeople.

One of the biggest limiting beliefs proprietors have been the belief that they receive their share of referrals.

John Jantsch of Duct Tape Marketing says 79.9% of business owners and sales professionals surveyed admit to having no system for getting referrals.

Those that do have referral programs do them incorrectly; these programs are not truly a system. Want to really build a successful referral marketing system? Want to lower your cost of acquiring a client or patient?

> ➢ Give them a reason to do business with you rather than someone else.

> ➢ The one area you can do that with, that you have the greatest control over, and that you can get the biggest return for your effort and money is strengthening your business relationships.

> ➢ Formalize your relationship capital management protocols.

The most sophisticated salespeople will cheerfully pay more for a referral.

For Additional Learning

BOOKS REFERRED TO IN THIS BOOK:

The Four Agreements: A Practical Guide to Personal Freedom by Don Miquel Ruiz

80/20 Sales and Marketing: The Definitive Guide to Working Less and Making More by Perry Marshall

PRODUCTS AND SERVICES OFFERED FROM...

Professional Leveraged Communication Solutions and the Author

Marketing For Salespeople the Online Course

Marketing For Salespeople Audiobook

Coaching and Strategy Sessions. For those who are:

- ➤ Trying to make sense of all their thoughts, ideas, and opportunities for their business.
- ➤ Wanting to launch something new for their business, or who wants to stop doing too many things and instead focus.
- ➤ Not sure what their unique selling advantage is, the kind of clients you should go after, how to package your services, etc.
- ➤ Not in love with their business or things that are not working, and you are not sure why or what to do about it.

Consulting. For those who:

- ➤ Need knowledge or execution support.
- ➤ Already know what they need to do but need advice on how to do it.

- ➢ Want to learn something new, like email marketing or writing sales letters.

- ➢ Want expert guidance on how to do something specific, like train referral partners or approach influencers.

Coaching. For those who:

- ➢ Need to work on their mindset or behaviors to better reach your goals.

- ➢ Have behaviors, like procrastination, which are holding you back from doing your best work.

- ➢ You want to leverage their sales career and become an intrapreneur or entrepreneur.

- ➢ You want someone to hold you accountable and talk through your concerns regularly.

For products and services offered through Professional Leveraged Communication Solutions please visit:

www.Marketing4Salespeople.com

UNLEASH YOUR POTENTIAL

Download Your Free Bonus Special Report Now

In the fast-paced world of sales, one skill stands out as the linchpin of success: Critical Thinking. We understand that mastering this art is the key to elevating your salesmanship and unlocking your full potential. That's why we're thrilled to offer you an exclusive opportunity to download our free bonus special report: "The Art of Critical Thinking: Unleash Your Potential and Elevate Your Salesmanship."

In this power-packed report, we delve deep into the strategies that transform ordinary sales professionals into strategic thinkers. Uncover the secrets to dissecting challenges, making informed decisions, and anticipating client needs with precision. Elevate your sales game by developing a razor-sharp mind that turns obstacles into opportunities and objections into triumphs.

Picture yourself effortlessly navigating complex client interactions, foreseeing objections before they arise, and positioning yourself as the trusted advisor clients seek out. "The Art of Critical Thinking" isn't just a report; it's your gateway to a new dimension of salesmanship—one where you become the master of your sales destiny, equipped with the tools to tackle any challenge that comes your way.

Ready to transform your approach and elevate your salesmanship to unprecedented heights? Don't miss out on this exclusive opportunity! Scan the QR below to download your free bonus special report now:

Seize this chance to equip yourself with the strategies that top-performing sales professionals swear by. The time for transformation is now. Download "The Art of Critical Thinking" and embark on a journey to unleash your potential and elevate your salesmanship.

To your success!

Warm regards,

Valdez Lasartemay

May I ask you a favor?

Dear Reader,

I am writing to express my deepest gratitude for choosing to embark on the journey through "Marketing for Salespeople." Your commitment to enhancing your skills in the ever-evolving field of sales and marketing does not go unnoticed.

As you've reached the conclusion of the book, your perspective and insights are incredibly valuable. Your engagement with the content signify a shared passion for professional growth and a commitment to excellence in the selling profession. Now, I invite you to take a moment to reflect on the impact the book has had on your understanding of marketing strategies tailored for sales success.

I am eager to hear about your key takeaways, the strategies you found most applicable, and any 'aha' moments that resonated with your professional journey. Your review has the power to guide and inspire others seeking to elevate their skills in the realm of sales and marketing.

If you could spare a few moments, I would be immensely grateful if you could please share your thoughts by leaving a review through the provided link

below. Your feedback will not only contribute to the ongoing improvement of the book but will also play a pivotal role in fostering a community of professionals dedicated to the principles of servant leadership in sales.

Your generosity in sharing your thoughts will not go unnoticed, and I genuinely appreciate your support in helping to grow a culture of professional servant leadership within the selling profession.

Thank you in advance for being an integral part of this journey, and for your continued commitment to excellence.

Warm regards,

Valdez Lasartemay

Marketing Strategist

INDEX

financial goals 58, 59

First Impressions 2, 25

freebie seekers 14, 15

G

Golden Rule 68, 69, 101

H

high-value thinking 97

I

ideal client profile 72, 145

ideal client referral partners 126

importance of networking 121

industry trade magazines 111

influencers 77, 116, 117, 118, 119, 120, 121, 122, 126, 130, 131, 132, 140, 141, 142, 153

institutionalized marketing 15, 18

insurance companies 18, 19

L

leadership philosophy 147, 148

leadership style 147, 149

LinkedIn 111, 122

Long game strategy 120

M

marketing activities 69, 94, 99, 133

marketing acumen 5

marketing approach 54

marketing avenues 127

marketing challenges 28

marketing copywriting 108

Marketing departments 15

marketing education 138

marketing efforts 15, 148

marketing experts 16

marketing managers 15

marketing message 145

marketing plans 19

marketing power 43

marketing professional 8, 49, 52, 72, 130

marketing promotion 109

marketing tactics 72, 73

Marketing Tool 147, 148

market niche 43, 44

Media kits 136

Michael Spinks 30, 31

Mike 30, 31

modes of 108, 110, 111, 122

motivational speaker 64

Myers 76, 77, 78

N

T

U

V

W

Y